1000
DAYS OF REVOLUTION

CHILEAN COMMUNISTS
ON THE LESSONS OF
POPULAR UNITY
1970-73

PRAXIS
PRESS

1000 DAYS OF REVOLUTION
CHILEAN COMMUNISTS
ON THE LESSONS OF
POPULAR UNITY
1970-73

ISBN 978-1-899155-07-1

Published by Praxis Press, 2018.
Email: praxispress@me.com

Distributor: Unity Books, 72 Waterloo Street, Glasgow, G2 7DA, Scotland, Great Britain
T: +44 141 204 1611
E: enquiries@unitybooks.co.uk
www.unitybooks.co.uk
www.facebook.com/unitybooksonline/

Originally published as "ONE THOUSAND DAYS OF REVOLUTION
CP Chile Leaders on Lessons of the Events in Chile" by Peace and Socialism International Publishers, Prague, 1978. General Editor K.I. Zaradov

Published with the permission of the Communist Party of Chile, Santiago, Chile.

Printed by Lightning Source

Contents

Introduction

Kenny Coyle

On the morning of 11 September 1973, British-made Hawker Hunter jets bombed La Moneda presidential palace in Santiago, Chile. Hours later, Chile's elected head-of-state President Salvador Allende was dead. Throughout the day, soldiers raided working-class districts across the country rounding up known left-wing activists. Around 40,000 were incarcerated in Chile's National Stadium, awaiting interrogation. Many faced torture and imprisonment, others execution. Hundreds of other militants simply "disappeared". Allende's government of Popular Unity was replaced by a military junta headed by General Augusto Pinochet.

The experience of the Popular Unity government and its dramatic and bloody end is dealt with in detail in the pages that follow. This book contains nine chapters, each one written by a prominent Chilean communist as part of their party's attempt to self-critically analyse the errors and weaknesses of Popular Unity as well as its achievements and successes; *1000 Days of Revolution* provides a balance sheet of that fateful period.

These articles were originally published in the Prague-based monthly *World Marxist Review,* an international theoretical and discussion journal of the communist and workers' parties, and subsequently published as a single book in 1978.

Apart from Rene Castillo's opening chapter, which was published in 1974, the other chapters date from around 1977. There have been some minor corrections in the translation to conform more closely to the original Spanish version and some explanatory background notes have been added.

The Chilean experience was a sustained attempt to advance to socialism through a non-armed strategy based on a constitutionally elected government.

Popular Unity's failure has often been taken by its leftist critics as definitive proof of the impossibility of any such path. Other commentators drew opposite conclusions, stressing the need for a purely "democratic road" to socialism instead, one that would seek compromise and consensus between mass political forces and differing traditions rather than through the intensification of class conflict.

The conclusions reached in this volume reject both these extremes. Specifically, they stress the confirmation of two fundamental insights of Marxism-Leninism. First, that the left cannot simply take over the existing machinery of government and the state inherited from and shaped by the existing ruling class. Second, that no successful revolutionary movement can hope to succeed unless it can consolidate and maintain a definite political majority among the population at large.

Leftist critics of Popular Unity tend to heavily emphasise the first factor, reformist critics the second. In reality, they are complementary elements and are fused within all revolutionary processes. Popular Unity's defeat was due largely to the failure to resolve these inter-related questions in time.

Defining Popular Unity as a revolutionary movement is not simply to take at face value the claims of its participants. This was also the view of its enemies, within Chile and outside. Reformist governments that simply tinker with established systems are rarely targeted for violent overthrow, on the contrary, their existence can sometimes act as a release valve to defuse potentially explosive social discontent.

Key economic changes, above all the nationalisation of the copper industry, sent shock-waves all the way to Wall Street and the White House, where the fear was that the Chilean experiment would be repeated elsewhere unless it was stopped – at any cost.

Roads to socialism

Chilean communists had always been greatly influenced by the international communist movement's experience and theories. Two consecutive conferences held in Moscow had set out conditions for the success of the peaceful or unarmed path of revolutionary struggle. The first meeting, in 1957, was attended by 12 of the communist and workers' parties then in power, while the 1960 event was much broader, bringing together 81 ruling and non-ruling parties from across the globe.[1]

Far from envisaging a "parliamentary road to socialism", as its ultra-left critics tried to suggest, the formulations used in both Moscow declarations were far more cautious and qualified. While a peaceful development of the revolutionary process was considered preferable to one involving the bloodshed of civil war, in which working people would always pay the heaviest price, it was acknowledged only as a possibility not as a certainty.

There was a decisive shift in the international balance of forces following the defeat of Nazism in 1945 and the subsequent creation of a socialist camp stretching from the Baltic to the Pacific.

This was a significant positive factor, inhibiting the potential for direct imperialist military intervention – as had happened in Russia following the October Revolution of 1917. A further positive development was the accumulated experience of the anti-fascist struggles of the peoples of Europe combined with those of the anti-colonial and anti-imperialist national liberation movements in Asia, Africa and the Americas.

In these arenas, the banner of democracy, progress and national independence had been raised by forces inspired by communist and socialist leaderships. Here the working class had cemented alliances with peasants, intellectuals and other middle strata. On occasion, broader coalitions had been built with democratic and nationalist sections of the bourgeoisie and their followers.

However, the 1960 statement laid out clear guidelines that were considered necessary to turn the possibility of a non-armed path into reality. In each case, the ultimate criteria were to be each country's specific national and historical conditions, not universal or timeless formulae.

Conditions of success

In summary, the world communist perspective on any successful peaceful, or non-armed, road was dependent on several factors:

1] The need for a firm alliance between the Communist and Socialist parties, representing the united front of the working class.
2] Winning over a majority of the people for revolutionary change.
3] Smashing "the resistance of the reactionary forces".
4] Securing a "solid parliamentary majority" for the left.
5] Transforming the existing mechanisms of bourgeois parliamentary systems to make these bodies representative of progressive social forces.
6] Creating mass movements of political struggle outside parliamentary structures.
7] Implementing economic measures "to ensure the transfer of the basic means of production to the hands of the people".
8] Promoting a programme of "class struggle of the workers, peasant masses and the urban middle strata against big monopoly capital, against reaction".
9] A readiness to shift, modify or even abandon peaceful forms of struggle in the face of reactionary use of violence against the popular forces.

While some of these features were present during the Popular Unity period, a number of elements were either missing or undeveloped.

Problems of leadership

The creation of Popular Unity was a remarkable achievement, bringing together as it did Marxists, radicals, secularists and Christians.[2] However, as Gladys Marin pointed out: "one of the main problems of the Chilean revolutionary process was that no solid and homogeneous revolutionary leadership was brought into being. At the same time, the gains that were made were largely due to the process of forming such a leadership. The main role in its formation and development was played, due to the very nature of the revolutionary process, by the working class, and to the extent that the working class failed in this respect, it made things easier for the enemy."

The unity of the Communist and Socialist parties was more highly advanced and longer established than in most other countries. Nonetheless differences of emphasis, pace and direction emerged, sometimes these were successfully resolved – but at other times they became a source of friction.

The nature of the Chilean revolutionary process itself was also understood differently by the forces within Popular Unity. While many in the Socialist Party and other left groups saw Chile as undergoing a fully mature socialist revolution, the Chilean communists categorised the initial stage of the revolutionary process as being national democratic in content.

For the Communists, this meant that revolutionary measures in the first instance should be directed not against private property in general but focused instead on foreign imperialism and the domestic oligarchy, whose monopolistic exploitation of the economy not only set them against the working class and peasantry but also against the mass of the middle strata and even sections of the small and medium bourgeoisie. If not all of these forces could be successfully rallied behind Popular Unity, at least efforts had to be made to neutralise them and prise them away from the camp of the far right.

In addition, the powerful example of the Cuban Revolution of 1959, inspired some sections of the left, both inside and outside Popular Unity, to transplant the Cuban experience of armed struggle, or at least their narrow interpretation of it, to Chilean soil.

Winning a majority

Starting with little more than 36% of the vote in the 1970 presidential elections, Popular Unity faced constant challenges to win over, or at least neutralise, the sizeable middle forces that were also being courted by the far right.

This was not an arithmetical challenge but a political one, as communist theoretician Volodia Teitelboim stressed: "We have said that the peaceful path is practicable only if the idea of the revolution wins the minds of the majority, of the people and prompts it to act. When the forces favouring change have achieved overwhelming superiority no opportunities are left for a reactionary rising, let alone for its success. The idea of majority, which Lenin considered so important ('the majority of the people are for us,' he said in September 1917), retains its validity as a requisite of victory whatever the form of struggle."

A destabilising factor was the shifts within the middle strata, a significant social sector given the undeveloped level of Chilean capitalism. These strata were closely linked to the Christian Democratic Party. The Christian Democrats took over a quarter of the votes (28%) in the 1970 presidential poll. They also retained significant working-class influence, with just over a quarter of the total votes cast in the main trade union federation in 1972, but its leadership also had close ties to big business.

Initially, the Christian Democrats were temporary allies in confirming Salvador Allende's presidency and supporting the nationalisation of the copper industry. However, over the course of the 1000 days of the Popular Unity government, the Christian Democratic leadership shifted into a formal alliance with the far-right National Party, creating the Confederation of Democracy in 1972. Together this anti-Popular Unity coalition hoped to secure a two-thirds majority in parliament. This could have allowed Allende to be impeached and removed from office, and also for other constitutional changes to be pushed through to the detriment of Popular Unity. However, despite the mounting difficulties, the March 1973 elections saw Popular Unity increase its share of the popular vote to around 44%. It added to its seats in both the Senate and Chamber of Deputies at the expense of the right and centre.

The vacillation of the middle strata is also illustrated by the fact that two successive left splits from the Christian Democratic Party, the first MAPU in 1969 and the second, the Christian Left in 1972, entered the ranks of Popular Unity. Travelling in the opposite direction, the Radical Party suffered right-wing splits to the opposition.

Parliamentary and extra-parliamentary conflicts

Those who accuse Popular Unity of following a "parliamentary road", over-look the fact that at no point did President Allende command a majority, solid or otherwise, in either of the two chambers of the Chilean parliament. While the 1973 parliamentary elections denied the right-wing a sufficient majority to use parliament to oust Allende, Popular Unity's minority coalition was unable to transform parliament into a forum more representative of the class forces it represented. This was also true in other governmental and state institutions.

Orlando Millas wrote: "the Party constantly warned against the danger posed by the euphoria of those who imagined that the September 1970 election had guaranteed the development of the socialist socio-economic formation. At a time when we had won power only in part, it was essential to democratise every field of activity, to carry out far-reaching democratisation measures in economic management, extend democracy to the judiciary and the control machinery, achieve a balance of forces in favour of democracy among the military and bring the administrative; system into line with genuinely democratic standards. We stopped half-way in this respect. The Popular Unity government failed to establish effective democracy in decisive fields. Its gains, while impressive and highly noteworthy, were clearly inadequate."

These weaknesses prevented Popular Unity from successfully advancing new forms of popular power. Jorge Insunza wrote: "The main thing, then, is to see to it that people can express their will and effectively exercise power 'from below', that they take a direct part in building the new democracy. Without this, the 'power at the top' cannot carry out its revolutionary tasks in the face of the embittered opposition of the reactionaries.

"In Chile mistakes were made in this respect. There was not enough clarity and unity among the revolutionaries regarding the type of state that had to be created, or the form and content of democracy."

As we know from declassified transcripts of meetings in Washington, involving the "40 Committee" US President Richard Nixon, National Security Adviser Henry Kissinger and CIA representatives, among others, regularly met to discuss US interference in Chile long before the election of Allende.[3] However, tied down in the war against the Vietnamese people, direct military intervention was not an appealing option. Instead, the US funded right-wing groups, sought out informers and contacts within the armed forces, and encouraged schemes to disrupt the Chilean economy.

Imperialist sabotage

Pedro Rodriguez noted: "In Chile imperialism did its utmost to destabilise the popular government. Economically it resorted to a financial and techno-logical blockade. With the help of Chile's financial clans it mounted desperate opposition inside the country, boycotting production, leaking currency abroad and speculating in capital. To this the imperialists and reactionaries added psychological warfare to intimidate the population, particularly the middle strata, create a black market, cause a shortage of consumer goods and food, and general economic chaos and anarchy. The imperialists and reactionaries were bent on preventing any balance of forces being established that would in any way be favourable to the popular government, and on isolating the latter."

The deployment of psychological warfare is taken up in the chapter by Rodrigo Rojas: He conceded: "We failed to give battle to the class enemy in the field of social psychology, nor did we use it to muster our own revolutionary forces. We are more aware now of the vast importance of taking account of the elements of the social psychology of the masses when analysing concrete situations. The founders of Marxism-Leninism always pointed out these factors as a permanent component of a scientifically grounded policy."

By mid-1973, following Popular Unity's stronger than expected showing in the parliamentary elections, there was growing frustration in Washington at the inability of the Chilean right to defeat Popular Unity through electoral means, despite generous US support.

Forms of struggle

Inside the country, the far-right began to despair of blocking or ousting Allende by peaceful means. Now the counter-revolutionary forces outside and inside the country turned decisively toward military action. In these circumstances, the forces of Popular Unity were unprepared to modify their strategy.

In the view of Volodia Teitelboim, the focus on solving the many practical problems emerging from Popular Unity's non-armed choice had obscured the need to make concrete plans for a strategic shift toward armed defence as conditions deteriorated. He argued: " 'Peaceful transition' is a correct term only in so far as it rules out civil war. But because of the many vicissitudes, it cannot bypass the law which says that violence is the 'midwife' of history. We should have always borne this in mind, should have remembered that the very act of changing path presupposes 'changing horses' and continuing our advance. It is hard to change horses in mid-stream. But then it is harder still when no preparations have been made beforehand," Teitelboim concluded.

Military failures

Repeated in differing formulations in the pages that follow, the downfall of Popular Unity was first and foremost a result of political defeats, the later military blows came only once a political atmosphere had been created that allowed the coup to succeed.

Hindsight fuses what in reality were two separate questions. Was the defeat suffered by Popular Unity on 11 September 1973 inevitable? The second issue is whether Popular Unity's chosen strategy could have successfully opened the road to socialist transformation had it survived or blocked the Pinochet coup.

The two are clearly interlinked but the first challenge was immediate and tactical, while the second was longer-term and strategic. After all, Popular Unity had previously blocked right-wing provocations, both civil and military, and had faced down the "Tancazo" in June 1973. Why was it unable to effectively counteract the military conspiracy later the same year?

Luis Corvalan, general secretary of the Communist Party of Chile, who had been a political prisoner of fascism before he was freed in an agreement with the Soviet Union in 1976, writes: "First, the Party did a good job in charting its political line for the whole period that led up to the partial winning of power, and for the first period of popular government. It is clear today, however, that our line for winning complete power and moving on to the next stage of the revolution, which would have enabled us to reach socialism, was not well enough worked out."

This political weakness led the vulnerability of armed action against the government, Corvalan believed since: "we did not evolve a proper military policy. Since 1963 the Party had been giving its members military training and making efforts to acquire enough arms to defend the government that we were confident the people would set up. But this was not enough, because our activity in this direction was not accompanied by the main thing, namely persistent and sustained propaganda to give the popular movement a correct attitude to the military. This was essential to dispel the military's incorrect, slanderously inspired notions of the working class and Popular Unity, to bring the ideas of Marxism to people's minds in an undistorted form. It must be admitted that the enemy, on the contrary, was continuously active in the armed forces."

Revolutionary experience

These articles were written, of course, before the varied experiences of Nicaragua's Sandinista Revolution (1979) and Venezuela's Bolivarian Revolution, begun in 1999. These events have added rich and complex features to Latin America's revolutionary history. They were also written nearly 20 years before the Pinochet dictatorship, faced with mounting popular discontent and splits within Chilean ruling circles, was cast aside.

After his fall Pinochet remained close friends with Margaret Thatcher and other leaders of the British Conservative Party, a fact that might suggest that the commitment of the British ruling class to upholding democratic forms of government is more a matter of expedience than principle. The failure of the then British Labour government in 1998 to put the dictator on trial or to extradite him to Spain for his crimes was a shameful act.

It would be wrong to take Chile's experience in 1970-73 as illustrating each and every possible challenge that revolutionary and left governments will automatically face. There are nonetheless sufficient common and recurring features to encourage today's generation of activists to learn lessons from the past. To do so, it is essential to study in detail the specific characteristics of each and every revolutionary process, situating them in their unique national and historical contexts. *1000 Days of Revolution* sets out to do precisely that.

NOTES

1 The relevant section of the statement reads:

"The Communist Parties reaffirm the propositions put forward by the Declaration of 1957 with regard to the forms of transition of different countries from capitalism to socialism.

The Declaration points out that the working class and its vanguard — the Marxist-Leninist Party — seek to achieve the socialist revolution by peaceful means. This would accord with the interests of the working class and the people as a whole, with the national interests of the country.

Today in a number of capitalist countries the working class, headed by its vanguard, has the opportunity, given a united working-class and popular front or other workable forms of agreement and political co-operation between the different parties and public organizations, to unite a majority of the people, win state power without civil war and ensure the transfer of the basic means of production to the hands of the people. Relying on the majority of the people and resolutely rebuffing the opportunist elements incapable of relinquishing the policy of compromise with the capitalists and landlords, the working class can defeat the reactionary, anti-popular forces, secure a firm majority in parliament, transform parliament from an instrument serving the class interests of the bourgeoisie into an instrument serving the working people, launch an extra-parliamentary mass struggle, smash the resistance of the reactionary forces and create the necessary conditions for peaceful realization of the socialist revolution. All this will be possible only by broad and ceaseless development of the class struggle of the workers, peasant masses and the urban middle strata against big monopoly capital, against reaction, for profound social reforms, for peace and socialism.

In the event of the exploiting classes resorting to violence against people, the possibility of non-peaceful transition to socialism should be borne in mind. Leninism teaches, and experience confirms, that the ruling classes never relinquish power voluntarily. In this case the degree of bitterness and the forms of the class struggle will depend not so much on the proletariat as on the resistance put up by the reactionary circles to the will of the overwhelming majority of the people, on these circles using force at one or another stage of the struggle for socialism.

The actual possibility of the one or the other way of transition to socialism in each individual country depends on the concrete historical conditions."

2 The main parties of Popular Unity were: the Chilean Socialist Party (PS), Communist Party of Chile (PCCh), Unitary Movement of Popular Action (MAPU), Radical Party, and the Christian Left (from 1972).

3 See the extensive range of documents published in *Foreign Relations of the United States, 1969–1976* Volume XXI Chile, 1969–1973, Editors James McElveen, James Siekmeier. General Editor Adam Howard. United States Government Printing Office, Washington, 2014.

About the Authors

RENE CASTILLO
Member of the National Leadership, Communist Party of Chile*

VOLODIA TEITELBOIM (1916-2008)
Teitelboim joined the Communist Party in 1932 and was a member of both the central committees of the Communist Youth and Communist party in the late 1930s. He became a member of the political commission of the PCCh in 1945. He lived in Moscow from 1973-78 organising clandestine radio broadcasts, *Escucha, Chile* ("Listen, Chile") among other tasks. He was a lawyer, prolific writer, poet as well as a Marxist theoretician. From 1961-73, he served as a senator and a deputy in the Chilean parliament. He was president of the PCCh 1989-94.

ORLANDO MILLAS (1918-1991)
Journalist and writer, Millas was a government minister for agriculture as well as economic reconstruction during Popular Unity. He won election three times as a deputy to the Chilean parliament 1961-73.

JORGE INSUNZA (Born 1936)
Joined the Communist Youth in 1955 and later the Communist Party of Chile. He was secretary of the Communist Students in 1957 In 1962 he became a member of the Central Committee and its Political Commission in 1965. Between 1965 and 1969 he was editor of the party newspaper *El Siglo* and was editor of the party magazine *Principios* between 1972-1973. After the 1973 coup, he was a member of the clandestine leadership of the Party between 1973-1976; member and coordinator of the Party in Europe; and member of the internal leadership of the Party between 1984 and 1989. He served as a deputy in the Chilean parliament 1969-73.

GLADYS MARIN (1937–2005).
Marin's father was a peasant and her mother a schoolteacher. In her early years, she was active in Christian youth movements and then joined the Communist Youth in 1958, became a Central Committee member of the Communist Party in 1960 and general secretary of the Communist Youth in 1965. She served as a member of parliament in 1965-1969, 1969-1973. After the coup, as a prime target of the military dictatorship, she was instructed by the party to leave the country. She took refuge in the Dutch embassy, while her husband Jorge Munoz stayed with their two children. Munoz was later arrested by the fascist secret police DINA and was never heard from again. In 1978, she returned to Chile to lead the party's clandestine work. She became general secretary of the Chilean Communist Party in 1994. When she died in 2005, the government declared a day of official mourning.

PEDRO RODRIGUEZ
Member of the National Leadership, Communist Party of Chile*

RODRIGO ROJAS
Alternative Political Commission member, Communist Party of Chile.*

MANUEL CANTERO (1925-2010)
Joined the Communist Youth in 1945. He served on the Communist Party's Central Committee and Political Commission in 1962. He was elected to the Chilean parliament for his native Valparaiso three times between 1965 and 1973. After the coup, he spent some years in exile before returning to Chile to join the party's clandestine fight against fascism.

LUIS CORVALAN (1916-2010)
Corvalán became involved in the communist movement aged 15. He was later elected member of the PCCh's Central Committee and after 1958 served as the party's secretary-general. He was imprisoned several times during the periodic repressions directed against the Communist Party. He was a senator from 1961-73. Corvalan was a political prisoner after the 1973 coup and was awarded the Lenin Peace Prize (1973–74). After a prisoner exchange between the Soviet Union and Chile in 1976, he rejoined the PCCh leadership. Corvalán returned to Chile in 1988.

* Positions held in 1978

Salvador Allende

1

The First Critical Analysis

Rene Castillo

The military-fascist coup of September 11, 1973, which overthrew the popular government of President Salvador Allende came as a profound shock to progressives everywhere. The powerful worldwide campaign of solidarity with the Chilean people is one of the most vivid manifestations of internationalism in the history of the workers' movement. It was given added impetus by the unparalleled wave of savage repression with its toll of tens of thousands killed and arrested and hundreds of thousands blacklisted.

The conscience of humanity was wounded by such atrocities and the voices of democrats throughout the world merged into a mighty chorus of protest.

There is another reason why the solidarity movement has attained such proportions: the universal interest in the Chilean experience, in the successes of the working-class and popular movement, which won the 1970 elections, formed the government, and had paved the way to power without resorting to arms.

The international working class, millions of people, were deeply interested in the success of the revolutionary process in Chile. The Chilean experience was not, of course, a model to be blindly copied. Yet it showed for all to see that in our time the working class, the people can advance to power within the framework of the bourgeois state, even under a reactionary regime. But only if there is a powerful revolutionary movement capable of acting in alliance with different sections of society and bringing about the democratisation of political life, consolidating democratic freedoms and achieving a balance of forces capable of preventing reaction from obstructing the revolution by armed violence.

The revolutionary process in Chile struck a responsive chord among revolutionaries and democrats throughout the world, especially in Latin America, which is just why imperialism did everything to doom it to failure and halt it.

Against a background of expanding Yankee monopoly aggression aimed at perpetuating their domination in what they considered their Latin American "backyard", Chile became the target of specially fierce attacks. As far back as 1970, a "working group" of the National Security Council was set up in Washington to draw up detailed plans of aggression against our people.

Imperialism gave its all-out support to the putsch or, to be more precise, to the numerous coup attempts against the Popular Unity government. The purpose of this support became apparent from the vicious reactionary press campaign that followed the overthrow of the popular government.

The *El Mercurio* newspaper, mouthpiece of imperialism and the big monopolies, repeatedly emphasised the international significance of the Chilean people's defeat. Voicing the thoughts and plans of the reaction, it wrote: the coup has worldwide implications, for in Chile it proved possible to reverse the Marxist revolutionary process, which is, as a rule, irreversible. Communism has suffered a defeat. It has been crushed on its second strategic front: on September 11 the legal path failed in Chile."

A curious argument! The self-proclaimed champions of "law and order" boast of destroying democratic institutions. They are in ecstasy over the bloodbath they unleashed; for them, the tragedy has paid off.

Critical analysis

The events in Chile are certainly a bitter, if temporary, defeat. It is only natural, therefore, that a number of questions arise which revolutionaries must answer. What did the people and revolutionary leadership do to avert the coup? Why was the fascist dictatorship able to consolidate in a few days while the armed resistance, justified and necessary at the time, proved ineffective?

Does the Popular Unity's defeat mean that the premise that power can be won without armed conflict is invalid in general or, at any rate, for Chile? These are but a few of the questions. To supply the answers signifies not only readiness to assume responsibility for what has happened (which is the duty of revolutionaries to our people and the world working-class movement), but also to analyse and chart the course to our main objective today: bring down the fascist dictatorship and eradicate fascism in our country once and for all.

Of course, no critical analysis will ever be final. New facts and viewpoints will continuously appear on different questions. That is why these contributions are not meant to conclude the debate, which is of such importance to the revolutionary movement. The Chilean people's victory in 1970 was the culmination of an intense period of mass battles on all fronts of social struggle. And the victory was possible because the people had rallied behind a policy which correctly defined the nature of the Chilean revolution and singled out the main enemies: imperialism, the monopolies and landed oligarchy. That was the main line of the attack.

The working class formed a socio-political front, the Popular Unity alliance. It promoted a correct overall policy which at decisive junctures helped win the cooperation of other social forces against reactionary plans. This policy made it possible to form the government, that is, win the most dynamic and important element of political power. From this vantage point, in a situation marked by bitter confrontation with the old ruling classes, the popular movement launched a process of revolutionary change in Chilean society. The changes had been stipulated in the Popular Unity programme in accordance with the character of the specific stage of the revolution: the prime need was to overcome backwardness and poverty and eliminate foreign domination and oligarchic rule.

This required the broadest unity and, at the same time, provided the basis for cooperation with forces outside the Popular Unity bloc, for their forward movement. At the end of 1970, CPC General Secretary Luis Corvalan defined the prospects as follows:

"The priority task now is to strengthen the unity of the people which can and should become an invincible force in advancing the Chilean revolution and the interests of the various classes and sections of the population, isolating reaction, thwarting its subversive plans, preventing foreign interference, rebuffing imperialist pressure and building up wide support for the new government. This is a crucial task, and it has to be accomplished in the very near future."[1]

Such measures as nationalisation of the big copper mining industry, creation of a public sector through nationalisation of big monopolies, turning the banks into state agencies, reactivation of the agrarian reform, redistribution of incomes in favour of the working people, progress in housing, public health and education, on independent foreign policy and, especially, broad popular participation in shaping the nation's future through a stronger and united trade union movement – all this is testimony to the profoundly national, popular and revolutionary character of the administration headed by Salvador Allende. Despite the temporary defeat, these achievements are an invaluable heritage of the Chilean people. And though wiped out now by the junta, they will forever serve as an example and inspiration to the working people and the nation.

Why did this process, objectively so in keeping with the interests and aspirations of the majority of the people, suffer defeat?

Firstly, because to foreign capital and the local oligarchy, which had enjoyed every imaginable privilege for more than 150 years, anything short of halting it would mean loss of power and wealth forever, a prospect they refused to accept.

The events in Chile fully confirm the Marxist position that moribund classes do not relinquish power of their own free will. Quite the contrary, they will fight tooth and nail. Nor does the fact of the working class winning a part of political power by unarmed struggle alter that. We must never forget what Lenin wrote in his *The Proletarian Revolution and the Renegade Kautsky* of the efforts of reactionaries who have suffered defeat: "For a long time after the revolution the exploiters inevitably continue to enjoy a number of great practical advantages: they still have money (since it is impossible to abolish money all at once); some movable property – often fairly considerable; they still have various connections, habits of organisation and management, knowledge of all the "secrets" (customs, methods, means and possibilities) of management, superior education, close connections with the higher technical personnel (who live and think like the bourgeoisie), incomparably greater experience in the art of war (this is very important), and so on, and so forth.

"If the exploiters are defeated in one country only – and this, of course, is typical, since a simultaneous revolution in a number of countries is a rare exception – they still remain stronger than the exploited, for the international connections of the exploiters are enormous. That a section of the exploited from the least advanced section of the middle peasant, artisan and similar masses, may, and indeed do, follow the exploiters has been proved hitherto by all revolutions, including the Commune (for there were also proletarians among the Versailles troops, which the most learned Kautsky has "forgotten")."[2]

This fully applies to our country. Matters were further complicated by the fact that the reactionaries held strong positions in the state apparatus, parliament, the judiciary and the mass media.

Taking advantage of all this, they launched an all-out war against the popular government, a war to the bitter end. Their use of different means of struggle is most instructive for our people and, we hope, other peoples.

Here are some examples. The reactionaries opposed the popular forces, especially the Communists and Socialists, under the banner of freedom and democracy. But as the class struggle gained in intensity they rode roughshod overall democratic institutions that clashed with their interests. If such institutions allowed the people to take over the reins of government or win a part of political power, they were railed at and vilified by their erstwhile defenders. The bourgeoisie may denounce terror "on principle" when in power, but it readily invokes terror, makes it its policy, when this fits its purpose.

The Chilean experience convincingly demonstrates that only the working class and the people are capable of preserving and developing the democratic institutions. In our time revolutionary processes, the advance to socialism, are the only genuine guarantees of political democracy. The struggle for democracy is inseparable from socialist development.

When power is won without armed struggle the ruling classes naturally seek to take advantage of "legality" in their fight against the revolution. But this is the same "legality" which justifies the revolutionary government in the eyes of broad sections of the public. It becomes a factor in facilitating, to a certain degree, revolutionary change and the marshalling of forces. Insofar as this is a transitional stage, the old government institutions are temporarily retained. But the revolutionary movement should not lose sight of the fact that the democratic institutions inherited from the old system are of a class nature, and democratic development inevitably entails changing the class character of the state. That is the only way to assure the advance of the revolution.

The enemy tries to exploit the situation by using government institutions where he still dominates to do away with those which no longer promote his class domination. This is where our government made a number of mistakes, which enabled the reactionaries to take advantage of democratic freedoms to create conditions for a fascist coup d'état, doing away with democracy altogether. Idealistic notions of freedom and an approach to problems without reference to the class struggle were a major negative factor. As a result, the fascists were spurred on by our tolerance of their activities.

Ideological confrontation is of special significance in a struggle involving the winning of a part of the political power in the framework of a bourgeois state system. The ideas of the outgoing classes continue to influence, more, to dominate, the masses. In addition, the reactionaries have the means of propagating their ideas: the press, radio, television, cinema, schools. All this is a powerful weapon of bourgeois restoration. If they are to succeed, the popular forces must crush the enemy on this front too.

We were unable to eliminate the disproportion between the reactionary and progressive mass media. Moreover, we did not make proper use of the opportunities at our disposal, whereas the enemy was quick to launch a campaign of slander and vilification, and mislead broad sections of the people.

From the moment the working class and the people take over, economic policy and activity are decisive in strengthening and extending their positions in the struggle for power. The reactionaries, on the other hand, having lost political power, do everything to plunge the country into chaos. Thus, the monopolists and landlords immediately launched a campaign of economic sabotage, undeterred by the harm this would cause the country and, in fact, their own interests (which to them are more important than those of the country). The aim was to create difficulties for the government at every step.

Reactionary resistance
The economic problems inherited from the past (a huge foreign debt, backward agriculture and underdeveloped infra-structure) were aggravated by these reactionary manoeuvres. As a result of the revolutionary process, demand, especially for consumer goods, formerly determined by capitalist relations and the corresponding distribution of income, increased, largely due to the increased needs of the society.

The revolutionary leadership has the task of improving living conditions for the labouring people, boosting production and labour productivity and fostering conscious labour discipline in the working class. The solution of these problems makes it possible to repair the damage caused along with reactionary resistance, by boycotts, sabotage, speculation and black marketeering, and, what is most decisive, improve the conditions of the masses.

In such an economically backward country as Chile these problems were especially acute, and we proved unable to resolve them successfully. Internal and external reaction managed to cause chaos and provoke a grave economic crisis, which was aggravated by our mistakes and weaknesses. This to a large extent explains our defeat.

The reactionaries used every means at their disposal to combat the popular government. Two opposing centres of power became clearly defined on all fronts of the class struggle and the bitter fight to gain the upper hand.

For the people to win in this confrontation it was essential for the working class to step up its revolutionary activity and at the same time show a greater capacity for allying with other forces.

Whatever the political circumstances, the prime need is to win over the overwhelming majority of the people and thus isolate the main enemies. This is borne out by the experience gained in the revolutionary process, the experience of victories actually won.

The success of 1970 should be seen in a broader light than just victory at the polls. The Popular Unity alliance actually won 36.3% of the vote. This made it the major force in the society, especially in view of the limitations of bourgeois democracy, which prevent the broad participation of the working class and the people in political life. But it was still only a plurality.

The election victory was consolidated in the bitter mass battles of September and October 1970 which ensured that Salvador Allende, who had amassed the largest number of votes, could be sworn in as President of the republic. Relying on national democratic traditions and taking advantage of contradictions between various bourgeois groupings, the Popular Unity alliance achieved joint action with other democratic forces, notably the Christian Democrats. In these battles the popular movement managed to tip the scales in favour of the revolution and rally the majority of the population against the main enemies. This made it possible to foil the attempted coup d'état of October 22 in which the Army Commander-in-Chief, General Schneider, was assassinated.

Political objectives

Thus, the 1970 victory was a triumph of the majority, and not only because the Popular Unity represented, and stood for, its interests (which is, of course, true of every working class, popular movement), but also because that majority identified itself with the political objectives of the Popular Unity in the specific conditions and helped achieve them. Without this victory would have been impossible.

To win the majority for ensuring the success of the Chilean revolution meant rallying broad public sections around the working class, whose alliance with the peasants is decisive in any revolutionary process. But although acceleration of the agrarian reform contributed substantially to the alliance (always rather a weak one in the history of Chile's class struggles), its strength remained insufficient in the struggle for power.

In the conditions prevailing in our country it was also necessary to rally broad middle sections around the working class, in one form or another winning over various non-monopoly bourgeois groups, notably the middle and petty bourgeoisie. And when we succeeded in achieving unity with these sections or their majority, bringing them together on the basis of concrete slogans or actions, we were able to win decisive revolutionary victories. The first of these was the inauguration of the popular government.

By that time, however, there were contradictory assessments of the situation. This prevented proper leadership of the popular movement and, in the end, became a determining factor in the defeat of September 11.

The Popular Unity parties and movements believe that the defeat was due mainly to the absence of a united leadership pursuing a principled policy and avoiding the pitfalls of "Left" and Right opportunist deviations. In this respect solid unity of Socialists and Communists is decisive. It is the guarantee of the monolithic unity of the working class and in the political front as a whole.

In Chile, Socialist-Communist unity goes back 20 years. It was steadily strengthened in the three years of popular government and is today stronger still. But, of course, there were difficulties. And there were gaps. Before the popular government they were bridged without serious damage to the movement, but in the crucible of the class struggle that followed the people's victory, they made themselves more painfully felt. For there were harder problems to tackle and the enemy took every advantage of our differences.

Both parties bear responsibility for the insufficient solidity of their unity. We do not deny our shortcomings, the sectarian evil within our ranks, notably in our local branches. This prevented fraternal discussion of problems and agreement on many questions. The class character of our Party, its better organisational facilities, imposed a greater responsibility on us in the face of the sectarianism displayed by our opponents.

The Communist Party of Chile is a working-class party. However, our leadership of the proletariat and the people and the fulfilment of our vanguard role presuppose cooperation with the Socialist Party, which likewise has important positions among the working people. This is a correct orientation, expressive of the unity of the revolutionary forces of the proletariat and petty bourgeoisie. And there are ample facts to bear this out. But this should not have precluded a more or less open statement, when and where necessary, of the fundamental views of the working class.

We discussed matters at leadership level and explained our class position. But we were not doing enough at local branch level, among the people. And yet such work could have prevented the spread of petty-bourgeois revolutionism which militated against Socialist-Communist unity and the revolutionary process as a whole.

A factor that worked against united leadership was the ceaseless subversion of the ultra-left elements against the Socialist-Communist alliance and the Popular Unity. Their aim was to create an avowedly anti-Communist "revolutionary pole" to replace the "reformist leadership" allegedly imposed by our Party. And their views met with response among some Socialist Party members.

Petty-bourgeois pseudo-revolutionary groups propagated the dogmatic concept that he who is not a proletarian or semi-proletarian is an enemy. The bourgeoisie, all of it without exception, was denounced as the "ruling class". This ignored the very real fact that the monopoly and agrarian bourgeoisie, those allies of imperialism, played a dominating role in Chilean society. They placed an oppressive burden on the proletariat, but also on definite groups of the bourgeoisie and on broad sections of the urban and rural middle strata.

This dogmatic concept also disregarded the dependent character of Chilean capitalism and the concentration of capital. Yet both one and the other are distinctive features of imperialism and produce the social contradictions the working class must always take into account in charting its political course and choosing its necessary and possible allies.

These ultra-left concepts did grave damage to the popular movement. More, they became the basis for a primitive ultra-leftist policy vis-a-vis the government. Everywhere they provoked clashes with small and middle entrepreneurs and instigated the seizure of factories and real estate of no real economic importance. They fostered a sectarian attitude towards the intermediate strata.

As a result the working class was gradually forced into isolation and the intermediate strata became, objectively, allies of the country's main enemies. In the fight for power there thus developed a balance of forces unfavourable for the Popular Unity.

Politically, the ultra-left rejected all compromise and alliances. Typical of their activity and views was their patently distorted picture of the Christian-Democrats, a mass party which in the 1973 elections polled about 30% of the vote (with 85% of the economically active population going to the polls). The Christian Democrats represented many classes, their influence extending to part of the proletariat and peasantry and also to part of the monopoly bourgeoisie. The party was strong among the middle strata. Nonetheless it was treated as a solid reactionary mass. This eminently suited the reactionary bourgeoisie and its leader, ex-President Eduardo Frei, helping them unite the party around a confrontation with the popular government. This, in turn, helped the putschists, with whom Senor Frei and his group were openly cooperating in the hope of regaining at least part of their lost power.

Another manifestation of ultra-left sectarianism was persistent rejection of alliance with the patriotic section of the army that remained loyal to the Constitution. This weakened its position and made it easier for the fascists to win over the officer corps and, in the end, block all resistance within the armed forces. Ideologically, dogmatism found expression in virtual disregard of the gains of popular rule. The Allende government was branded reformist and there were calls for mass struggle against it. In fact, a section of the working people were drawn into it by a propaganda cocktail of banal economism and pseudo-revolutionary phraseology.

It has to be said, however, that some problems – pertaining to education, for instance – were wrongly approached. This complicated the government's relations with the Church, whose most influential spokesmen took an objective stand and were sympathetic to the government's social reforms a fact that has immense importance.

We know from history that such actions are bound to produce a receptive soil for opposition sentiments and for fascistisation of part of the petty bourgeoisie and other middle strata.

The Chilean experience has reaffirmed anew that ultra-leftism is a boon for imperialism and reaction, which assiduously cultivates it as a means of defeating the people. The opportunist essence of the "Peking Leftists", too, stood out in Chile in all its ugly nakedness – even in the eyes of the petty-bourgeois pseudo-revolutionists. The Leftists ended up by extending a hand of friendship to the fascist putschists.

The shortcomings of leadership mentioned above gave elbow-room not only to ultra-leftism, but also to manifestations of Right opportunism. In fact, both of these ideological deviations often came from one and the same social and political centre.

One of the most pronounced features of the Right deviation was economism which sank deep roots among the more politically backward groups of working people. Speaking for our Party, its General Secretary declared that, with a people's government in power, the well-being of the workers depends not only, and not so much, on the success of actions in support of their demands, but on the destiny of the Popular Unity government, on the achievement of its goals.

The bourgeois parties egged on the workers to put forth excessive demands in the hope that this would erode the government's social basis. Worse still, the ultra-lefts – and indeed elements in the Popular Unity itself that had succumbed to their influence – were working in the same direction. The demands were couched in pseudo-revolutionary phraseology. The forces behind them were concerned solely for their narrow party interests and for extending their influence. Little did they care that by inciting some groups of the working people against the government they were abetting the putschists.

Ultra-leftism

They refused to acknowledge the necessity for subordinating the fight for economic demands to the struggle for power. As was only to be expected, the response come chiefly from the politically immature workers of small and medium enterprises, with little or no militant traditions. And so, various forms of economism helped to alienate the intermediate strata.

All this affected the attitude of these groups of workers in the battle for more production and higher productivity. And that was a battle the government had to win to strengthen its position and resolve the issue of power in its favour. But the ultra-lefts were telling the workers that "economic problems and production should not take precedence over the class struggle" and that "the big capitalists should see to the growth of production". In this induced atmosphere of boycott and sabotage, the Leftists urged the masses to abandon all efforts to resolve this crucial problem which, in the final analysis, would determine the country's future. They would have nothing to do with the major tasks we had set. Their sole concern was to win a cheap popularity by flattering the masses. And so, ultra-leftism and right-opportunism merged.

The Chilean revolutionary process was harmed also by manifestations of bureaucracy, survivals of a non-proletarian attitude to the state apparatus and lack of faith in the people. There was a definite trend to "assimilate" the part of the state apparatus we took over following the 1970 election victory: use it without making any changes whatsoever. This conflicted with the attempts to restructure the government machine notably by giving the people a bigger part in running it.

Needless to say, no previous Chilean government had allowed the working class and the people anything resembling the opportunities we provided for planning and controlling the affairs of society. Without going into the shortcomings, we must ask to what extent fulfilment of this task accorded with the demands of the revolutionary process and the pace of changing the class character of government institutions.

Bourgeois government begins and ends with bureaucracy. We revolutionaries possess tremendous reserves for multiplying our forces and making our work more effective. These reserves are the working people, when they are enlisted to perform the functions of government and to set up an "extremely intricate and delicate system of new organisational relationships extending to the planned production and distribution of the goods required for the existence of tens of millions of people".[3]

Consistent accomplishment of these talks called for deep faith in the masses and for class firmness. To eliminate bureaucracy, the Communists made it a point that government officials should not enjoy any privileges. Our officials were paid a modest salary and everything above that went into the exchequer. We also introduced stringent rules to prevent corruption or any propensity to draw advantages from one's official position. Hundreds of workers were placed in executive posts and we did everything to give the working class and the people a bigger share in running the country. However, the results were anything but satisfactory. We committed mistakes. Take, for instance, the system of worker-participation in management, which operated parallel with the trade unions. It had originated with the workers, but was meant for another, and to a certain degree, contradictory function. This slowed down the real involvement of workers in management and gave rise to a harmful tendency within the trade unions. Their role was now reduced to advancing economic demands, and they had no part whatever in management. We began to set things right, but only after the damage had been done.

In sum, all these varieties of "Left" and Right opportunism exerted a definite, in some cases a decisive, influence on the popular movement and weakened the positions won in the battle for power.

Our Party said in its first appeal to the people after the fascist coup: "The Communist Party is absolutely confident that its policy of unreserved defence of the Popular Unity government, its steps towards mutual understanding with other democratic forces, especially at basic level, its efforts to inspire confidence in the middle strata, its striving to direct the main blow against the main enemy, ie, imperialism and internal reaction, its perseverance in strengthening the alliance of Communists and Socialists, unity of the working class and mutual understanding of the Popular Unity parties, its struggle to increase production and raise productivity, to put state-run factories on a paying basis, its campaign for higher labour discipline – all these were components of a fully correct general policy. But this should not be taken to mean that there were no shortcomings and errors."

Though our policy won wide acceptance and though a substantial part of the working class and the people worked with dedication to achieve the goals of the revolution, we were not able to unite the whole popular movement on this basis.

Indeed, the Popular Unity was unable to prevent isolation of the working class or to win over the majority of the population, whose vital interests were inseparably linked with the success of the popular government. This predetermined the victory of counter-revolution in the battle for power. We suffered both military and political defeat (military defeat was due mainly to our political defeat). We were defeated because the working class was isolated from its allies.

Working in close contact with President Allende and consistently promoting unity of all participants in the Popular Unity, our Party made every effort to resolve the issue of power without recourse to armed struggle. We were working on the premise that, in all cases, the path to power presupposes active mobilisation of the masses. The success of the revolutionary process is inconceivable without struggle. It takes the strength of the masses to suppress the resistance of the reactionary forces that always confront the people who are working to achieve their aims. It takes the strength of the masses to prevent violence by a real or potential body of reactionary power. The possibility of success on the non-armed path to power (sometimes referred to as the peaceful path, but that is not a quite accurate definition) implies the masses' ability to detect and check attempts to unleash reactionary armed violence. That possibility emerges in a definite set of historical circumstances, and increases if the relation of forces becomes more favourable for the people and if the reactionary forces are increasingly isolated.

Alignment of forces

And we can look back on major victories in working towards that aim. It will be recalled that, after Dr. Allende's election, imperialism and the oligarchy tried to prevent his inauguration. When this failed they tried to overthrow his government. For three years the Chilean people thwarted the plots of the CIA and ITT (October 1970), of Major Marshall (March 1971) and of General Canales, the lorry-owners' strike, the strike of shopkeepers and members of the liberal professions (October 1972) and the abortive coup of Colonel Souper (June 1973). In all these cases the people's victory over the plotters was possible because the alignment of social forces created by the activity of the government, the parties and the masses favoured Popular Unity.

In contrast, the September 11 coup was possible because imperialism and internal reaction had built up a broad anti-government front. This was its class composition: the monopoly bourgeoisie and agrarian oligarchy made up its core and it included the vast majority of the middle and petty bourgeoisie, most of the middle strata, the backward elements of other social groups. Its political composition: the putschists had won over (besides the reactionary parties) most of the Christian Democrats led by Frei, and the right elements that had broken with the Radical Party. The military make-up: the putschists were able to involve the vast majority of servicemen and police and prevented practically all action in defence of the democratic government.

This became clear a few hours after the coup was launched. At first there was organised popular resistance in many places. Many members of the Communist and other Popular Unity parties fell in this heroic struggle, fighting with whatever weapons were at hand. But the working class and the people, the leadership of the revolutionary parties and President Allende realised that it would be madness to bring all our forces and reserves into this unequal battle.

The President told the people of his decision and the reasons for it: "In this great ordeal I will pay with my life for loyalty to the people. Force is on the side of the enemy and he can win. But neither force nor criminal action can halt social processes. The people must defend themselves but they must not commit suicide. The people cannot allow themselves to be trampled upon and destroyed, but neither can they allow themselves to be humiliated. This grim and bitter hour will be survived by others. I am confident that I am not giving my life in vain."[4]

It is hardly necessary to comment on the dignity of these words and the revolutionary devotion expressed in them. But it is important to understand that the President regarded the political situation as extremely unfavourable for the popular forces.

Political defeat

And it is in this sense that we assess our defeat primarily as a political one and only after that as a military one. The isolation of the working class from its allies enabled the reactionaries to launch their coup. Isolation ruled out the possibility of the working class and the people taking up arms. We officially state that there could have been such a possibility, but only if it were not tantamount to mass suicide.

The tragic outcome of this stage of the Chilean revolution requires an analysis also of our attitude towards the armed forces. The September 11 coup showed that the putschists had compelled the Chilean armed forces to break with their long-standing tradition of non-interference in politics and to betray their professional duty and loyalty to the democratic institutions.

The popular movement relied on these traditions when it made its choice of revolutionary path. And we followed that path when the new government was in power, endeavouring to enhance the army's democratic traditions and strengthen its institutional character to foil fascist attempts to turn the military into running dogs of reaction.

We relied heavily on the army's professionalism, its respect for the elected government and we endeavoured to bring the armed forces into the work of economic development without in any way impairing their defence preparedness. At times of crisis we worked in alliance with the patriotic part of the army faithful to the Constitution, and this played a decisive role in suppressing the October 1972 conspiracy. This alliance could have developed, were it not for the spread of ultra-left conceptions.

Meanwhile the putschists continued their plotting. Officers true to the popular government were retired and by a series of treasonous acts reactionaries were installed in key command posts. The reasons why they succeeded are partly objective. They were able to carry out their plans, using the reactionary ideology injected into the armed forces, chiefly as a result of imperialist penetration, and the class composition of the officer corps. These factors grew as the isolation of the working class from its allies increased. The subversion was long and systematic, geared to an operational plan the carrying out of which began in 1972, according to recent admissions by Pinochet. All this culminated in the fascist coup.

We were not able to build up an adequate support base among non-commissioned officers and privates who, by virtue of their class origins, gravitated towards the popular government. To a certain degree there was a contradiction between our efforts to enhance the professional character of the armed forces and our work in explaining to servicemen what the Popular Unity government was all about.

Then, too, there were many illusions about the army's devotion to its professional duty and the Constitution. As a party we committed one of our most serious errors in overestimating the democratic nature of the government system and not taking timely steps to reorganise it. This applies also to the armed forces.

Such are some of the lessons of the tragic events in our country.

The fascist dictatorship brought in by the military coup has thrown the country back to domination by imperialism and the monopoly and landlord oligarchy. Chile is under a vengeful, ruthless reactionary regime uninhibited by the constitution or by law and maintained in power by force of arms. Its policy is an expression of its class character and fascist ideology. The junta usurped power by taking advantage of a political situation that was to the disadvantage of the popular movement; the majority of the population were not prepared for defence of the legitimate government. But after the first six months of junta rule its base has begun to disintegrate. Its policy is detrimental to the interests of the majority of the people and is rejected by it. Now no one has any illusions.

Politically, the junta has destroyed all forms of democracy. Its policy is one of mass repression, incessant and flagrant violation of elementary human rights and wanton destruction of all democratic freedoms.

The junta has abolished the constitutional state and replaced it by a police state. Our Party has emphasised that the military coup destroyed all the institutions, leaving only a decrepit judiciary and a puppet Comptroller-General. Both are purely decorative-the judges dutifully rubber-stamp sentences pronounced by the military tribunals and the Comptroller-General rubber-stamps military orders to give them the "force of law".

In culture and ideology, the policy has been to root out Marxism, all doctrines which, in the junta's view "serve to conceal or abet Marxism". That formula had been tried in the past by certain individuals, and we know what happened to them.

Fascism cannot, by a stroke of the pen, cancel out democratic traditions born in long and hard years of struggle. Nor can it stifle the people's love of freedom and their democratic customs, which have become on inseparable part of the national character. The people, above all the numerous, militant and organised working class, are not likely to give up their rights. Chile has a strong tradition of popular organisations, notably trade unions and political parties, to give expression to the people's will. Today this tradition is a cardinal factor of unity for democratic renewal.

The attitude of the Church towards the inhuman repression is highly indicative and of immense importance. Many prelates and priests have taken up the defence of the persecuted. They have even established a network of ad hoc relief committees and have called upon their congregations to take part.

The junta's arch-reactionary economic policy has come as a terrible blow to the majority of our people. It has shifted to them the cost of the economic crisis caused chiefly by the reactionary boycott and sabotage during the popular government and further aggravated by the world capitalist crisis.

Prices are growing at a fantastic rate, purchasing power is sharply declining. Politically-motivated dismissals are increasing unemployment, itself the result of the economic crisis. Unemployment is now spreading to the middle strata, the professions, and the petty bourgeoisie.

This policy favours monopoly concentration. Capitalist accumulation, accelerated through intensified exploitation of labour and impoverishment of the masses, has meant a shrinking home market. "Deficit enterprises", ie, those that cannot match the productivity level of developed capitalist countries, are being wiped out, the process being sped by abolition of protectionist tariffs and reduction of credit facilities. And all this to boost "free competition". In short, the country is being abandoned to the tender mercies of local and foreign monopoly capital.

The worst hit is the working class. Economic hardship is attended by an onslaught on the trade unions, a ban on strikes, even on petitions, attempts to liquidate the organised workers' movement, and so on. Junta policy is aimed also at the peasants, of whom thousands have already lost the land they gained in the past. Farm workers are doomed to a life of poverty.

The middle strata find themselves earning less and paying more taxes to finance monopoly expansion. Lastly, junta policy is sharpening the contradiction between the non-monopoly and monopoly bourgeoisie. "Free competition" has spelled ruin for most small and medium businesses. Junta policy and activity have absolutely nothing in common even with bourgeois reformism. There is no economic basis for a populist policy; the monopolies are gaining full control.

The junta's vaunted "nationalism" is manifested in typically fascist persecution of foreigners (political emigres, intellectuals, workers). This cannot conceal or obscure the fact that it dutifully responds to US imperialist diktat. The evidence: denationalisation of our national wealth, control of the economy by the International Monetary Fund – its observers give the orders, the "nationalists" carry them out.

In the post-coup political situation the basic contradiction remains that between the Chilean people and the united forces of the imperialists, the monopoly and landed oligarchy. The main enemies are the same; only their methods have changed: they are using fascism in a bid to bring back the privileges lost in the three years of popular government and re-establish their class domination.

In the new situation, the anti-imperialist and anti-oligarchic front takes on the form of an anti-fascist front comprising all who are sincerely concerned for the wealth of the nation and for the democratic values fascism wants to destroy. These forces will join the anti-fascist front also because their social and economic interests are in crying contradiction to the policy imposed by fascism. Concrete conditions will lead to the merger of the democratic struggle with the struggle for revolutionary transformations.

The revolutionary popular movement must base its policy on our-experience, on analysis of our victories and mistakes. It must avoid sectarianism, which not so long ago inhibited the working class in forming alliances. More, to be a sectarian in the choice of revolutionary path is to bring grist to the fascist mill.

Democratic renewal
In the present situation Socialist and Communist unity is basic to unity of the working class, the Popular Unity forces and the politically minded sections of the population. The Communist Party declared in a statement issued last December: "At the same time we must go further, towards united action with sections of the people, that did not see eye to eye with the popular government. In differentiating between the people and its enemies, we must look to the future, not to the past. For the line of division is not between the government and the opposition as it was prior to the coup, but between the fascist usurpers and those who suffer from their reactionary policy and are prepared to work for democratic renewal, progressive social change and national independence."

Popular Unity can play its role if closer mutual understanding within its ranks is achieved through fraternal dialogue and on a principled basis. That is crucial to overcoming past mistakes, working out a uniform strategy and tactics and joint leadership of the revolutionary forces. And there is within Popular Unity a definite trend towards closer understanding based on a principled policy, and within the different parties near-agreement on the need to concentrate on organising and uniting the masses. That is the only firm basis for the movement's continued development.

Another crucial question concerns more active Christian Democrats' participation in the anti-fascist front. There are two trends within the Christian Democrat Party: one cautiously criticises the junta, but only to induce it to take a more favourable attitude to the Christian Democrats even give them a share in running the country. But there are other, democratic popular groups that appreciate the need for social change, share liberation sentiments and incline towards an understanding with the left forces. Which of these two trends will prevail depends entirely on the Christian Democrats themselves. Their inner-Party problems do not directly concern us. What does concern us is the need to avoid sectarianism, which plays into the hands of the reactionaries, and to strive for unity so that the Christian Democrats may become full-fledged members of the anti-fascist front. That can be achieved: the objective basis is there, and the actions of our common enemies are broadening it.

The banning of the Christian Democratic Party, and closure of its press by economic and censorship pressure are generating resentment against the junta, which it is trying to suppress by more repression.

The anti-fascist front should also be open to unaffiliated left organisations, but there has to be agreement on the programme and methods of struggle and fraternal relations in all joint activity.

Democracy cannot be brought back without struggle. We understand active resistance to mean action by the masses united against the dictatorship. And such action has already begun: the workers' and popular movement is being reorganised, groups of workers are fighting for their rights. Of course, these are still rudimentary and sporadic actions, but they are important considering the general recession of the labour movement after the coup. Resistance is expressed also in solidarity with the victims of repression and in the new contacts that are gradually bringing the people together again.

Anti-fascist front

Building up a front against the junta is not easy. Common viewpoints have to be identified and practical solutions found for problems. As it develops, the anti-fascist front will draft a government programme: destruction of the dictatorial police state and creation of a new, law-governed, democratic, anti-fascist, national, popular, representative state that will resurrect democracy, eradicate fascism, introduce revolutionary transformations and assure the country's independence.

The appeal our Party issued shortly after the coup, in October 1973, emphasises that "the people will return to power but, of course, will be under no obligation to re-establish all the old institutions. The people will adopt a new constitution and new laws, will promulgate new decrees, establish new government departments and institutions as part of a law-governed state of a higher type than the one strangulated by the putschists. And it will be a state in which freedom of thought will be respected along with all the humanist principles, but there will be no place for laws leaving loopholes for economic sabotage, subversion and fascism".

Chile's time of ordeal is bound to influence its future. Institutions in which so many blindly believed have been consigned to the dustbin of history. Indeed, who is likely to stand up for the old judicial system, or for a parliament that signed its own death warrant?

And so, when we speak of democratic, anti-fascist renewal we have in mind not merely re-establishment of the pre-coup state of affairs, but wide and comprehensive development of democracy. The new institutions will effectively assure government by the majority, will oust all fascist elements, civilian and military, and will possess the means to scotch any attempt at a fascist comeback.

The new, anti-fascist state will guarantee a multiparty structure and the normal activity of all democratic parties. We want a multiparty government, a people's government even more representative than that of the Popular Unity. And it must be a strong revolutionary government to ensure stable democracy and rapid social progress.

The anti-fascist front must solve still another important problem, namely fundamental reform of the armed forces and the carabineer corps, without which there can be no democratic state.

The armed forces, which in the most brutal manner reversed the country's development, are now 'serving imperialist and oligarchic reaction. The generals and officers who helped involve the army in the plot against Chile and its people bear a terrible responsibility to history, and they will be called to account for all their crimes and all the bloodshed. They have destroyed the honour and prestige of the armed forces in the eyes of our people and the world. They have trampled on Chile's finest traditions and turned its armed forces into hangmen of the people. They are guilty of the greatest of all crimes, treason to their country.

Needless to say, we have never seen the social struggle as a confrontation between civilians and the military. Many servicemen were true to their patriotic duty, but were unable to prevent the terror against the people, and those who protested against the fascist coup and the repression have suffered at the hands of the junta. Many were executed after a hasty trial or without any trial. At this writing, dozens of soldiers, NCOs and officers are being tried. There is a public campaign to save their lives.

Chile needs armed forces that never, under any circumstances, will come out against the people and become the running dogs of the oligarchy and imperialism. Our 'Party's appeal cited above contains this passage: "After what has happened, the Chilean people have a right to organise an army and police of a new type or, at any rate, expel fascist elements from the army, police and investigative agencies in order to prevent a repetition of the present tragedy."

That is the goal and it is important that it should also be shared by democratically-minded soldiers, officers true to their professional duty.

On the other hand, political developments within the armed forces and the Carabineros (police) can prove a decisive factor in shaping the character and forms of the anti-fascist resistance. The junta wants a fascist-oriented and fascist-indoctrinated army. But the democratic and patriotic traditions, violated during the coup, are still alive and the fascistisation process is meeting with mounting resistance. And this against a background of universal dissatisfaction with junta policy and uncertainty about the future.

The popular movement has declared its determination to revive the democratic and patriotic traditions, counter junta policy and expose it in the eyes of the people. The fascists are desperately trying to consolidate their position by bribing officers with higher salaries (substantially higher than workers' wages, plus a 15% "internal war" bonus). The army is being enlarged, and this means more taxes. Yet, we are firmly convinced that the fascists will not prevail over the people.

As mentioned above, the battle for broader democracy intertwines with revolutionary transformations. There can be no gap between the two when it is a question of the working class leading the anti-fascist front.

But its leadership has to be based on closer unity. Though the organisation of the anti-fascist front is a process of unity and struggle, the victory of the revolution will be assured only if the working class follows an independent policy, carefully explaining it – and not imposing it – to other social strata. Contradictions within the front are a logical development, but they must not be allowed to acquire an antagonistic character.

The working class can play the leading role if it wins over the greater part of society. But this, in turn, requires alliance with broad social strata. Hence, the anti-fascist front can operate only through mutual understanding. And this will be all the greater, the stronger the working class and the higher its revolutionary activity.

A revolutionary must help deepen social contradictions not in some abstract form, but in the context of the sharpening basic contradiction. Acting in this way we can merge the struggle for democracy with that for revolutionary change, for broad alliances and for making the working class the centre of unity, the motive force and guarantee of far-reaching revolutionary changes.

Decisive here is the ability of the working class to use slogans and forms of struggle that unite all the democratic forces, its ability to pursue a principled policy that rules out right and "left" opportunism.

Political maturity

A revolutionary situation can be brought about only by a mass movement that takes account of the concrete problems facing the people. Forms of struggle emerge in the course of this process. The revolutionary leadership organises, generalises and-applies them, without, however, ignoring the level of political maturity of the masses, the real correlation of forces and the need to improve it by every step we take.

Slogans must fully accord with the tactical aims of each stage in accumulating the revolutionary forces. They must be brought to the masses; and we have to distinguish between strategic and tactical propaganda and agitation slogans, always consider the interconnection between the various slogans, never confuse them.

This means that individual terror, adventurism and conspiracy must be rejected by the popular movement. All the evidence shows that the fascists would be only too happy to see actions of this kind, to justify the terror on which their power rests. In the past terror and provocation were deftly exploited by the enemies of the people. They could cause even more damage now, considering the nature of the present regime. The major forces of the popular movement, particularly the Communists and the Socialists, have already stated their views on this issue.

On the other hand, our Party believes that there should be no hard and fast framework in the battle against fascism and for a new government: this would not contribute to the revolutionary process. But we do believe that certain comment is called for.

First, it must be emphasised that the experience of the class struggle in Chile – and this includes the terrible temporary defeat – confirms rather than refutes the theory of revolution elaborated by the international workers' movement. Despite the claims of the reactionaries and the representatives of petty-bourgeois revolutionism who echo them, the non-armed winning of power in certain countries and under certain conditions has not been invalidated by the fascist coup in Chile. By the same token, the temporary defeat of a national movement seeking to capture power through armed struggle does not signify that such a revolution is doomed to failure.

In Chile, the possibility of non-armed winning of power has obviously diminished compared with the position before 1970. Elections as a form of struggle for political power have to be ruled out for an indefinite period.

On the other hand, the fascist dictatorship is more likely to react to the mounting public resentment by fresh attempts to keep the people in submission, even at the price of civil war. And it might well unleash such a war against a mounting mass movement to topple the regime-its unparalleled cruelty confirms that supposition. In that case, armed action by the people will become necessary. Its forms may differ, depending mainly on the role of the working class. However, the more probable possibility is a nationwide rising rather than guerrilla warfare.

The extensive opportunities for alliances open to the working class, precisely because the country is under fascist rule, create the prerequisites for an alignment of forces in our favour, and the reactionaries will hardly venture to use arms against an offensive by the popular forces.

Though democracy has been abolished, civil war is not the only form of such an offensive. A general political strike supported by the vast majority of the population can stay the hand of those who would use reactionary violence. Indeed, that was the case in Chile when its people got rid of the military dictatorship in 1931.

In other words, our Party is anxious to avoid dogmatic judgements, which can only harm the process of accumulating revolutionary forces and the process of democratic renewal. But we are also anxious to avoid petty-bourgeois pseudo-revolutionary formulas such as "power comes from the barrel of a gun". Power comes from the masses, though guns, obviously, play a part too, as we know from our own experience. But that experience has also taught us that guns shoot or do not shoot depending on the strength of the people. If the people are strong, united and prepared for struggle, they will find the means to prevent the enemy from shooting. That too, has been proved by revolutionary experience.

What we emphasise again and again is that, no matter what path of revolution we choose, the main thing is broad, full mobilisation of the masses and full utilisation of every opportunity to wage the struggle on every front, and rally more and more forces around the working class. That can be achieved all the easier if the revolutionary forces emphasise the close link between the democratic aims and socialist perspective of the Chilean revolution. That will help isolate fascism on all sectors of the front.

The main thing is concrete, day-to-day patient work among thousands of working people, women, and the younger generation, among all Chileans. That is the key to victory in any struggle.

No revolutionary process can be carried to completion if it does not have the support of the masses. Violence is part of every path to power by the working class and the people. But violence need not mean recourse to arms. It will depend on the character of the resistance offered by the reactionaries, or, more precise, on the character of the resistance they could offer. It will depend also on the activity of the proletariat, on the degree of isolation of its enemies, on processes within the armed forces, on the international situation, etc. And since these variables cannot be defined in advance, it would be wrong to draw up blueprints: they will lose all value as the revolutionary movement develops.

A few minutes before his death, the President, Comrade Salvador Allende, appealed to the people for the last time. He expressed deep faith in the forces of the working class and the people, the faith of a staunch revolutionary. "I am convinced," he said, that the seeds we have sown in the minds of millions of Chileans cannot be destroyed. Continue your work in the knowledge that, sooner or later men of good heart and courage will again open the road to a better society."[4]

We Communists are convinced of that. For there is no force on earth that can permanently hold back the revolutionary process, despite the present hard but temporary setbacks. We are deeply aware of our responsibility to the international workers' movement. And today as never before the powerful solidarity campaign in which democratic-minded people everywhere have joined, reinforces our determination to advance cooperation and unity with all revolutionary trends for victory over fascism. Our Party is prepared to exert every ounce of energy and to make every sacrifice in the fight against fascism. The junta is deliberately perverting the facts in an attempt to cast aspersion on the patriotism of Chilean Communists. The fascists are using every kind of savagery to break imprisoned Party members and active democrats. The usual method is to get them to confess to having committed crimes. That is done to undermine the militancy of the working class and the people. But nothing can break their resistance.

The fascists could not conceal the fact that Communists face the firing squad in firm confidence that the country and the Party, the cause of the working class and the people, will triumph. Even double-dyed reactionaries find themselves compelled to admit that they have failed to destroy the Communist Party, and are urging more and more repression. All their attempts to destroy the Party are doomed, including the slanderous allegation that our Party is split. Communist unity is becoming stronger than ever and there is a monolithic wall against enemy agents and fascist subversion. Thousands of Chilean Communists are working among the masses to strengthen their Party, inspired by the immortal doctrine of Marxism-Leninism. Ours is a Party trained by Luis Emilio Recabarren, Elijah Lafertte, Galo Gonzalez Diaz, Ricardo Fonseca, Pablo Neruda and thousands of others, and it is invincible.

Its fighting spirit has found expression in the words of our General Secretary, Luis Corvalan: "I am firmly convinced that we will come out of this dark tunnel to re-establish freedom and, at long last, our working people will take the place in history that rightly belongs to them."

NOTES

This article was published in 1974 and is one of the first attempts by the Chilean communists to summarise the lessons from the Popular Unity experience.

1 Corvalan, Luis "Chile: The People Take Over", *World Marxist Review*, December, 1970).
2 Lenin, *The Proletarian Revolution and the Renegade Kautsky*, Collected Works, Vol. 28, pp. 253.
3 Lenin, *The Immediate Tasks of the Soviet Government*, Collected Works, 4th English Edition, Progress Publishers, Moscow, 1965, Vol. 27, p241.
4 Salvador Allende, "Last Words to the Nation", radio broadcast. Transcript can be found here,
https://www.marxists.org/archive/allende/1973/september/11.htm

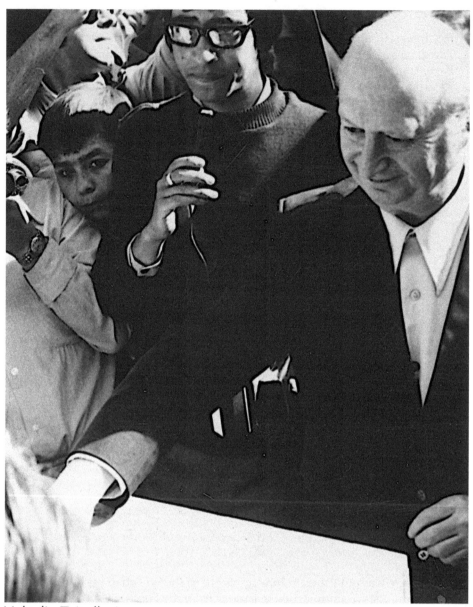

Volodia Teitelboim

2

Once More About the Events in Chile

Volodia Teitelboim

L enin took careful account of the lessons of the Paris Commune and the 1905-07 revolution in Russia to evolve on their basis the strategy and tactics which in 1917 led to the victorious October Revolution. Similarly, it is essential for Chileans to make a deep study of the 1000 days of Popular Unity rule, in all the diversity of its typical and atypical factors and features, and draw proper theoretical and practical conclusions. By analysing the highly valuable data at our disposal, we can – in a definite social microcosm, within the bounds of a small country of 10 million – ascertain the characteristics of a political drama of universal significance.

We can make a sober assessment of the achievements and miscalculations of the popular movement, of its correct moves and its mistakes. The evidence we have also makes it possible and necessary to study the enemy's methods and devices, to compile a veritable manual showing how present-day counter-revolution can strangle revolution.

To be sure, the only political value of such manuals. is that they point to a specific example governed by general laws, with all the peculiarities of place and time that characterise every revolution and every counter-revolution.

We will endeavour to examine the past impartially and self-critically, suggest correctives to our activity and reveal the overt and covert lines of enemy action, all of which is bound to make for greater clarity regarding our strategy and tactics, as well as those of the enemy. This will be the prologue to introducing corrections into our activity to transform the people's defeat into victory.

We think the events in Chile indicate, in the final analysis that, given definite circumstances resulting from a complex course of historical evolution and from a painstaking building up of forces and uniting all the strata striving for social change, it is possible to achieve through elections much more than an ordinary or even a considerable victory and, on the other hand, much less than real power.

Those events also show that no electoral victory holds a guarantee of its solidity. Such a victory can be a notable advance on a long and generally thorny path abounding in dangerous curves and crossings and often skirting a precipice. But unless victory in elections is followed up by a vast offensive of a popular majority to turn it into real power which the masses would be willing and able to hold and defend against all obstacles, against all attempts by enemies at home and abroad to ignore and do away with this power, the result may be, or is even bound to be, defeat.

Indeed victory in elections brings power only in part. Being the beginning of a new stage in the revolutionary process and the completion of previous stages, it does not come overnight but is a result of the revolutionary process as a whole, of a growing structural crisis in the country stemming from a deterioration of the general crisis of capitalism. It is the ultimate result of the accumulation of preliminary reflecting the maturing of diverse forms of class struggle.

That was how a pre-revolutionary situation shaped up in Chile. The Communist Party regarded elections as a form of action in the struggle to transform society, and in this it required winning majority support.

Forms of struggle

"Political majority" means something more solid and complete than a relative or absolute majority of votes. To a greater extent than an arithmetical (or mechanical) majority, it must be expressive of the greater part of the population. Besides, it must be an active majority, one not only operating continuously (which is typical of any steadily developing movement) but realising the need to uphold by every possible means possible the gains made.

Yet during the growing revolutionary process in Chile, the forms of the struggle were considered as its goals. Form was exalted to the rank of substance, as it were, and an absolute was made of one path. This was undoubtedly a mistake, for when the concrete situation changed, the masses found their hands tied.

While the peaceful development of the revolution was in keeping with prevailing conditions and expressed the will of the popular movement, it was far from being in harmony with the mood of an enemy ready to stop the revolution at all costs and by every means, including means that were anything but peaceful. This must be borne in mind. The enemy's bellicosity and aggressiveness should never come as a surprise to revolutionaries. The enemy will always do his utmost to put up resistance. He will grasp every chance to take up arms against the people.

Every phenomenon or development is dialectically influenced by diverse factors and every concrete truth has fundamental and secondary aspects. In the light of past events, we consider that in the case of Chile the political factor certainly played the main role in the interconnection of the political and the military factor.

The latter factor is a part of the former, but an essential one. Hence the immense significance of the military policy of the popular movement. It implies more than merely adopting a definite position towards the army and establishing a solid alliance with its potentially democratic part. It implies forming a force that could make common cause, as far as possible with the section of the army loyal to the revolution.

Experience has shown that our advance must be safeguarded not only by popular, but also by adequate military support. And the precondition for that is a constructive policy on this issue (with the Communists assuming special responsibility, of course).

It is vitally important, therefore, to restore the revolution (in our conception of it) to its highly dialectical nature, always bearing in mind that this is a process that can change depending on the course of the struggle, and that at times its evolution can accelerate to the point of dictating other forms of struggle, as was the case in Russia in 1917.

In other words, we must make no absolute of this or that path of the revolution, must not consider that the choice of the path is final and may not be revised, or that one and the same principle should be used invariably through a long period of history. Switching from one form of struggle to another in other countries may not take place as rapidly as it did in Russia in the few months preceding the October Revolution. But our negative experience suggests that it is wrong in general to attribute an unchanging character to any particular form of struggle, to treat it as a constant making it possible to disregard changes in the situation, often abrupt ones, caused especially by political crises and growing contradictions.

"Peaceful transition" is a correct term only in so far as it rules out civil war. But because of the many vicissitudes, it cannot bypass the law which says that violence is the "midwife" of history. We should have always borne this in mind, should have remembered that the very act of changing path presupposes "changing horses" and continuing our advance. It is hard to change horses in mid-stream. But then it is harder still when no preparations have been made beforehand.

Irrespective of how clearly the necessity for the change is realised, the very possibility of such a change and the ability to carry it out must certainly be guaranteed. This is not a matter that can be settled at the moment of change; it requires advance preparations, which may even take years, and this is what Chile's popular movement failed to do. The revolutionary vanguard marching at the head of the masses must be really prepared to adopt if necessary the most vigorous measures against a reactionary onslaught.

What happened in Chile under Popular Unity rule was that many regarded preparations for an eventual change of path and forms of struggle as absolutely unacceptable. Another lesson taught to Popular Unity is that an atmosphere of legality admittedly makes for stricter enforcement of laws and hence gives revolutionaries more strength and can, in the end, help them to make rapid progress but that in definite cases it can contribute to enemy plans for a rebellion or coup. Unless this is properly understood, legality itself may be used for tying the people's hands and making it even harder for them to exercise their right to legitimate defence. The people have no reason to feel bound hand and foot by legality like a Gulliver. They should regard it as a useful weapon in upholding their just cause, but never as a trap or gag.

In setting up the machinery of their conspiracy, reaction and fascism in Chile harped on absurd accusations against the Popular Unity government, saying that it had trespassed the bounds of legality. What they were after was to trample all legality underfoot (as if developing in their own way Odilon Barrot's statement, "legality is killing us",[1] they set out to implement the slogan, "Let us kill legality"). Developments showed, in particular, that they turned the arms control law into a trap for the people by using it to disarm and crush them.

All this confirms the need to respect a fundamental demand: reliance on the masses. We have said that the peaceful path is practicable only if the idea of the revolution wins the minds of the majority, of the people and prompts it to act. When the forces favouring change have achieved overwhelming superiority no opportunities are left for a reactionary rising, let alone for its success. The idea of majority, which Lenin considered so important ("the majority of the people are *on our side*," he said in September 1917), retains its validity as a requisite of victory whatever the form of struggle.[2]

Strategic unity

Consequently, the alignment of forces is of decisive importance. We must always, I think, see to it that the front of advocates of change is stronger than that of their opponents and that this superiority is considerable numerically and organisationally, as well as in terms of political, ideological, cultural, propaganda and all other activities. In other words, this broad front would be stronger in regard to the quality and solidarity of the alliance, to the dynamism and effectiveness of its united action. Also its programme must be the common denominator of all factors and the elements and forces making it up. On this basis, they must operate in coordinated fashion, on the principles of tactical and strategic unity, as they strike joint blows in one and the same direction. It is only in this way-by operating as a genuine coalition, avoiding the rise of opposed poles or disunited action inside the movement and by developing a common programme line-that the enemy can be defeated. The preservation and extension of the scope and strength of the front and the consolidation of the majority are a vitally important factor, as experience has shown, for the advance of the revolutionary process.

I repeat, the enemy will use force for as long as he can. The revolution can do without bloodshed, but only if the majority can impose this and the minority cannot prevent it. This could have been true of the period our country went through in the closing months of 1970 and partly in 1971. However, the enemy will always do his utmost to regain his strength. Hence it is not a question of only one moment of danger, for there is danger as long as there exist reactionary forces and it increases when reaction succeeds in reversing the situation in its favour.

Consequently, the problem of the balance of forces makes it necessary to take account of its inconstancy and likely changes. It is not established once and for all except when the revolution, having consolidated its positions, overcomes this internal contradiction and eliminates antagonistic classes to build a classless society.

Throughout the period of Popular Unity rule, Chile was under a kind of dual power, which cannot, of course, be compared to the situation in Russia in 1917. In Chile there was a lawful popular government and, on the other hand, an unlawful reactionary power backed by all who earlier had dominated society.

In addition to certain key economic and financial levers and the mass media, that reactionary power controlled a considerable part of the state apparatus. It skilfully exploited the miscalculations and incompetence of Popular Unity and the existence of different trends in it to bring the petty bourgeoisie into the effort to carry out reaction's plans.

This large social stratum is often undecided, being attached to its own values and frightened by the stories which the enemy's machinery of psychological terror continuously spreads.

The enemy knew full well that he would get nowhere unless he won the support of the intermediate strata and influenced the heterogeneous group of people differing in political consciousness, ideology and behaviour in the climate of hysteria cunningly created through the efforts of the CIA.

If the oligarchy made certain gains through its strategy of winning over the masses it was only because it had the support of other strata not belonging to its class. It succeeded in this because there was no adequate counteraction from the other side, that is, because the popular movement had no policy linking up with the programme of the movement and inspiring the intermediate social strata with confidence that they, too, would have a place in the new society.

The decisive factor for the outcome of the struggle in favour of the people is, undoubtedly, correct leadership of the popular movement, a leadership capable of giving the masses proper guidance, keeping them informed, mobilising them for this or that necessary action and making this political majority fully aware of its responsibility and turning it into a totality of politically conscious and united forces. Needless to say, the Communist Party plays an essential role in this, as do the other Popular Unity parties.

The Chilean popular movement doubtlessly has historic achievements to its credit and showed creative initiative throughout the period of Popular Unity rule. There developed rudimentary forms of democratic government that sprang from a people determined to change the class nature of the state, and that should be taken into account in the future as useful precedents of genuine democratic rule capable of keeping chaos under control.

However, Salvador Allende's assumption of the Presidency could not in itself alter the class nature of the state, the character of the armed forces, the police or the administrative machinery. This is why we stress that in any process following a peaceful course, it is most important to bring about an alignment of military forces in favour of revolutionary development. This is a key issue.

Popular Unity was faced with the pressing need to effect changes that would put the state apparatus under the people's organised pressure to the point of gradually placing it in the people's service. Furthermore, it was indispensable to promote active democracy involving the participation of the masses in the broadest sense of the term, strip the reactionaries of their spheres of domination and transfer all real power to the working people, to the progressive social strata.

There is no denying that in the three years it was in power, the Popular Unity government won the active support of the masses. However, confusion over the objectives – democratic or socialist ones – and the introduction of ideas alien to its programme, or based on sheer utopia made it impossible at any moment to give the initiative of the masses the right direction and secure majority support in solving every problem, as was the case with so patriotic a measure understandable to all as the nationalisation of the copper mines.

Let it be stressed that the sad conclusion of this chapter of history should not minimise the significance of so evident a reality of the past as the fact that in less than three years, the popular government mode tremendous progress by scoring valuable gains which live on in the people's memory and are part of a lasting political patrimony (even though they were subsequently destroyed by the fascist regime). They became a legacy that will again play an important mobilising role when the country has overcome its present state. It would be wrong to underestimate this experience. We must give serious consideration to the vastly positive significance and great constructive contribution of a popular movement that was broken off so tragically.

However, we maintain that unless the masses are constantly schooled in political action and in assessing the political situation, they cannot by merely following their instinct rise to the level of social awareness needed to defeat the enemy and participate consciously in making history. Hence it is a duty of the Marxist-Leninist political vanguard, of the Communists operating at home or abroad, to provide the working class and the popular movement with scientific leadership at any moment, even in the dire conditions of fascist rule. In fulfilling its fundamental mission, the Communist Party, the leading party responsible along with other parties, its allies, for the development of the revolutionary process, must solve a dialectical equation consisting of two elements: the quality of its unity with other forces of a popular movement not free of contradictions that can at times grow to dangerous proportions; and its independent role in this movement as a party which can under no circumstances, even amid discord, renounce its duty to present its policy to the people and country with a view to strengthening and not weakening unity

The positions of the representatives of the popular camp were undermined step by step, and eventually this became perfectly obvious and made for the success of the reactionary coup. Besides, there were shortcomings in the implementation of the working class policy of alliances and the balance of forces in both the political and the military spheres deteriorated noticeably in the closing months. For all this, however, the negative epilogue of this period of the Chilean revolution was not due, as has been said, to the people's will, but to the crippling forcible interference and violent change brought on by the fascist coup.

It is necessary that the revolutionary process be supported by a popular majority. On the other hand, while this factor is indispensable, it does not guarantee the success of the revolution, whose progress may be upset and its gains nullified if the popular movement is unable to support the resolve of the majority through effective defence measures.

We do not mean arms alone. To achieve political results, imperialism and home reaction launched their offensive first of all in the economic sphere, that is, a sphere in which they were particularly strong and in which they could do it all the more easily. The economic offensive was combined with individual terror, which by now has become a widespread daily practice of Latin America's political reactionaries.

Parallel policy

The resulting situation was one of utter chaos, described by some as very well organised. It was organised by the CIA, which did not hesitate to use for the purpose an all-out propaganda offensive. Perhaps it was the first time that counter-revolution had used the mass media so thoroughly, on so large a scale and with such force. This is another page of history worthy of most careful study. Reaction's plans were furthered by the government's failure to take coordinated and organised counter-measures. The existence of two parallel policy lines within Popular Unity contributed to the success of reaction's conspiracy. Besides, the conspirators continuously took advantage of the ultra-revolutionaries' talk about armed forces, which they did not have.

What we are trying to say is that a war in which no guns are fired requires a common, clear-cut policy that must constantly be spelled out to the masses. It is not merely a question of properly organising intelligence and counter-intelligence. The task is to carry on a total political struggle aimed at disuniting the central forces of the conspiracy from top to bottom and in every respect – economically and psychologically, publicly and otherwise, but above all militarily.

These bloody events cast a stark light on the role of the armed forces. Underestimation of this issue translated itself into a new tragedy for the people. What we witnessed was not a mere repetition of the past or a confirmation of the lessons of a long period of history. More than before, imperialism and its domestic allies are anxious to bring the army out of the barracks. This is due to the tacit admission that the development and growing strength of the popular movement more than ever endanger imperialist and capitalist control of society and the state. Revealingly, it is no longer a question of military actions, which have been numerous in the 150-year-long history of Latin America's republics, that is, of a conspiracy against a high-ranking adventurer, of a simple replacement of a power-thirsty individual in the government palace. As a rule, now it is a matter of outright action against the popular movement, taken above all when reaction has no other means of preventing a victory of progressive forces or abolishing their gains. This prompts us to reappraise the military question from today's point of view. No new approach to it is conceivable if we overlook the important fact that imperialism persistently seeks support among Latin American armies, which it tries to influence as on inseparable part of the forces implementing the Pentagon's global strategy.

According to an imported doctrine accepted by certain domestic military leaders, the chief enemy today is not outside but inside the country and is called "internal subversion". At a certain juncture, the US military-industrial complex evolved the tactical principle of Vietnamising the war, which expected "Asians to kill Asians". Its present motto in our country virtually expects "Chileans to kill Chileans", which means that the armed forces must wage war against their own people. This would make it easier for the imperialists to assure their domination and plunder of Chile. In this context, Pinochet's statement in Uruguay that he had acted in the interests of imperialism was brazen tragicomedy. "The United States," he said, "did not fire a single shot to remove communism from Chile. It was no Vietnam. No one was killed." Indeed, no US soldier was killed but then many thousands of Chileans were. Pinochet disregards these deaths.

Military training

Certain Pentagon political and military strategists have said that their best investment is training Latin American officers in US military academies and imparting Pentagon thinking to them. Indeed, this is what they have done. Senator William Proxmire announced in 1971 that between 1945 and 1971 – the US had spent US$175million on the training of 320,000 servicemen from 70 independent countries. In 1965, Robert Wood, then in charge of military aid, proudly said that almost all Latin American officers had received training in the United States or in the Panama Canal Zone.[3]

The imperialists are now reaping the fruits. In several Latin American countries, they have imposed reactionary military dictatorships in their service. And they are plotting to do the same elsewhere.

In learning the lessons of our own mistakes, we must therefore draw the following conclusion: to ensure that the revolution follows a peaceful course, we must prevent reactionaries in the armed forces from turning them into executioners and stranglers of the popular movement. In other words, we must see to it that the army stops playing the role of a super-police that it does not operate as a domestic colonial force taking orders from the Pentagon, an insurance company or a praetorian guard protecting the interests of monopolies and latifundium holders.

One of the greatest weaknesses of the Chilean popular movement was that this question was posed inadequately, narrowly and shyly as it were, preferably at the level of individuals, to the exclusion of parties having deep roots among the people, to the exclusion of the masses. For a long time, men shirking their duties remained in charge of the army and the police.

The sentiments of many high-ranking officers were little known (the case of Pinochet is the most striking, but not the only one). The information services, honey-combed with subversives, were disastrously incompetent. Besides, everything was affected by lack of unity in the government over the support for General Carlos Prats when he headed the cabinet and after his removal as commander-in-chief. It is our sincere opinion that we Communists, too, are to blame for that historical miscalculation, which was a result of the weakness and inadequacy of our military policy and our attitude to the armed forces.

How can a favourable change in the army be brought about? It is a very difficult task but undoubtedly a feasible one. To answer this question as correctly as possible, we must analyse the social nature of the army, its class composition and the mechanism of its activity, its changing functions in the course of history and its present role in society in other words, the dialectics of its behaviour.

The armed forces of Latin American countries are neither abstract institutions nor sinister organisations destined inevitably and for ever to brutally suppress their peoples. There is no need to stress here the special character of the revolutionary armed forces of Cuba, brought into being by a victorious socialist revolution. But even in the armies of those countries of the continent where there has been no revolution, we are witnessing developments that do not entitle us to a fatalistic interpretation of their role or to extreme pessimism.

Karl Marx distinguished two currents in the Spanish army (historically speaking, it bore a certain similarity to the armies of the countries of one-time Spanish America in atmosphere and as a school for the training and indoctrination of troops). He saw two incipient alternatives of social and political activity for it that manifest themselves to this day: an obtuse reactionary attitude and, at the same time, a potential for revolutionary initiative, as the rising led by [liberal revolutionary] Rafael del Riego showed.

This initiative can only manifest itself in periods of political crisis. Lenin pointed to the living connection between a developing revolutionary movement and its reflection in the armed forces, growing restlessness in the army. It must be admitted, however, that it was not this characteristic of the army that was the historic dominant, but the army's being the armed guarantee of a system based on oppression.

Chile had quite a few advocates of the theory of "particularism" of the army, who claimed that at a definite moment it adheres to "political neutrality". It is only right to point out that the army always acts under the decisive influence of this or that class or movement. It would be utopian to think of the army as being politically "neutral". Not so when, in a definite situation, a period of neutralisation is brought about as a result of struggle outside and within the armed forces to foil fascist plans aimed at involving the army in a reactionary coup. In this instance, the people can lean on those elements in the army that remain loyal to the constitution. Within the framework of the concept of peaceful development of the revolution, this neutralisation can have a certain effect for a time.

A very important factor to be borne in mind is, of course, the class origin of the military. However, the fact that most members of the armed services come ultimately from the working class and poor peasantry manifests itself on a mass scale only under the impact of a revolutionary situation and provided there exists an organisation in the barracks that is carrying on definite ideological work. The point is that a false social consciousness and a false conception of public duty are imposed on the military, or at least on many of them, and that this makes effective ideological and political work on our part all the more necessary.

According to a view commonly held by students of this problem, there was evidence of three currents in the Chilean army prior to the coup. They are classified – without sufficient scientific accuracy – as follows: (1) patriotic servicemen, or "constitutionalists"; (2) servicemen loyal to their professional duty, and (3) servicemen favouring fascism. This classification is more or less close to the truth and retains its validity. However, it would be mechanistic to overlook the changes subsequently brought about by the operation of internal and external factors. The struggle, including the ideological struggle, which, of course, is going on in Chilean society in spite of the monopoly of the mass media held by a totalitarian state, has its effect on the armed forces as well. The country's anti-fascist forces, its popular and democratic movement, can and should contribute actively to this struggle.

There are objective prerequisites for this: a deep-rooted, disastrous economic crisis; a political vacuum around the junta, the international isolation of the regime, and the hatred which the vast majority of the population feel for it. In the period since the imposition of the dictatorship, various subjective factors have been maturing too. The role of the working class has increased over the past year.

The Communist Party perseveres in its guiding role, braving savage repression. Its organisations are active throughout the country. The major popular opposition parties are reorganising at the national level. Discord within the ruling group is mounting. There is more and more evidence of vacillation in army circles, which daily witness growing condemnation of the junta by a population convinced that the military clique, far from solving any of the country's problems, has aggravated them. More and more people in the army condemn the unbridled terrorism and unprecedented brutality of the junta and the countless abuses by DINA. The activities of this agency, which depends directly on Pinochet, are marked by a sinister man-hunt and increasingly numerous lists of "missing persons" containing the names of prisoners of Chile's gestapo whose arrest the regime refuses to admit.

We know that hastening the end of today's nightmare, of the people's suffering, depends largely on ourselves, on the activity of Popular Unity and the anti-fascist forces generally. In drawing numerous lessons from the Chilean experience, many of which are bitter while others are instructive, and all of which are equally useful, we consider that by carrying on a selfless, extremely dangerous but increasingly widespread and organised struggle, the people will pave the way for changing the situation. This will make it possible not only to return Chile to its people when the time comes but to contribute to the elaboration of certain pressing theoretical and political problems.

NOTES

1 Odilon Barrot, conservative politician of the French Second Republic. His statement "Legality is killing us", betrayed the intention of reaction late in 1848 and early in 1849 to provoke a popular rising, quell it and restore the monarchy. See Frederick Engels, Introduction to Karl Marx, *The Class Struggles In France 1848-1850* Selected Works, Vol1, p. 202.

2 Lenin *The Bolsheviks Must Assume Power,* in Collected Works,Progress Publishers, Moscow, 1964, Vol. 26, p. 19.

3 See Fernando Rivas y Elizabeth Reimann, *Un caso de penetracion imperialista*. Ediciones 75, Mexico City, p. 7.

Congress of the Chilean Communist Youth (JJCC): Luis Corvalan (holding hat), Chilean Communist Party general secretary, next to him is Gladys Marin, leader of the Communist Youth and future party leader, along with international guests

3

Democratic and Socialist Stages and Tasks of the Popular Revolution

Orlando Millas

The tasks of the Chilean revolution are still valid. The democratic changes planned by the people in the recent past are more indispensable than ever. The establishment of a brutal fascist regime that turned back the country's development made it particularly evident to the vast majority of Chileans that none but a radical solution of the serious problems left unsolved would meet their interests and aspirations. This is not to say, however, that the inevitable return to these problems implies a repetition of the past. The tragedy of recent years has not been in vain.

We all learned much since the coming of fascism – both those who backed the government of President Allende and those who were opposed to it even though they shared many of its objectives and anti-fascist positions. At present all the problems appear in a new light. The need is for a broader coalition based on a superior conception. Hence analysis of what was done, of the gains and shortcomings of the revolutionary process of the 1970-73 period, far from throwing us back to the past, can help us to grasp the problems of the present and future.

A statement released by the Communist Party in Santiago in September 1976 said again that the chief task was to defeat fascism and restore democracy and that this task must unite and mobilise the whole people. It noted that the struggle for social freedoms and democracy is central to all revolutionary activity. The Communists' proposals are aimed at coordinated action by all patriots to bring down fascism. Furthermore, they envisage definite commitments to "build a more democratic political system than before, one that would grant more freedoms while preventing the restoration of fascism".[1]

Life has shown that the Communists were right in rejecting nihilist attitudes to democracy. Lenin's ideas regarding the importance of the struggle of the workers and the people for democracy are particularly relevant today. We view the democratic tasks and socialist objectives of the Chilean revolution in their dialectical unity and consider their realisation to be one process having its political and socio-economic stages.

The concept of popular revolution is the best definition of our process. As far back as the early 1950s, the Communist Party, drafting its Programme, subsequently approved by the Tenth National Congress, discarded the term "bourgeois democratic revolution". It held that such a term was likely to cause a certain confusion at a time when, with the rise of a financial oligarchy and the growing role of imperialism, the dominant policy of the bourgeoisie was acquiring an explicitly reactionary meaning.

However, the Party rejected a simplistic analysis of social contradictions. It pointed out that there were contradictions between the interests of the financial oligarchy linked with imperialism and those of other sections of the bourgeoisie. It expressed the opinion that the tendency to deny the differentiation going on among the bourgeoisie and prematurely attribute a socialist character to the process, far from helping to accomplish consecutively the tasks necessary to pave the way for socialism, actually made it more difficult.

Revolutionary stages

Classically, the revolutionary process has a democratic and a socialist stage. The names of these stages do not mean that they are entirely different; on the contrary, they stress their interconnection. Indeed, while no socialist tasks are set at the first stage, it sees the realisation of democratic tasks which afterwards are carried further and acquire a new content, with the result that there develops a democracy capable of serving as a form and instrument of the socialist revolution.

We regard the anti-imperialist, anti-oligarchic and agrarian revolution as the democratic stage of the advance to the socialist revolution. The Party's definition of the working class as "the centre and motor of revolutionary changes", which is determined primarily by the very nature of our epoch, the epoch of transition from capitalism to socialism and communism on a world scale, became a slogan of the working class, helping it to unite the masses in a struggle for goals meeting the interests of the whole people. Thus a powerful anti-imperialist movement led by the working class came into being, and parliamentary forms of struggle and political action merged with action by the masses.

This process itself took place against the background of international contradictions and in the context of their evolution. The role of democratic demands in drawing nearer to the socialist revolution became more pronounced. The character of bourgeois legality and bourgeois institutions was partially modified in the people's interests.

All this is inseparable from the fact that the Communist Party considered the possibility of the non-armed revolutionary path using also forcible means against imperialism and reaction, a vast variety of forms of struggle, with emphasis on fostering the revolutionary consciousness, unity and organisation of the masses and on the relationship of alliances. This theoretical proposition of the Communists that the revolution in our epoch advances along different paths was confirmed by a peaceful transition, so that major revolutionary democratic changes were envisaged and effected.

An important aspect of the revolutionary process was that Chile's workers and people were steeled in class struggles. They came fully to realise their strength, widened their political horizons, strengthened their will, fought their way to power and ruled the country for three years. They crushed a series of conspiracies and carried out far-reaching changes by nationalising the major copper and iron mines, transferring the saltpetre and coal mines to the state and establishing a public economic sector by socialising the banks, big monopoly-owned industrial enterprises, and the major foreign and home trade concerns. They accomplished an agrarian reform eliminating the latifundia and transferring the land to peasant cooperatives, redistributed the national income in the working people's favour and adopted an independent foreign policy. The people's participation in government was given a powerful spur.

The popular revolution in our epoch has both allies and dangerous, aggressive enemies. Fulfilment of the tasks of the democratic stage of the revolution arouses suspicion, hatred and aggressive hostility on the part of imperialism. The case of Chile dramatically confirms this. The fascist coup was openly directed by the multinational companies affected by nationalisation, in direct collaboration with the CIA and Pentagon. Internal reaction was galvanised by US imperialism, with its sinister plan to "destabilise" the Popular Unity government, defeat democracy in Chile and impose a fascist tyranny, an outspokenly terroristic dictatorship of the most aggressive forces.

The principal allies of every popular revolution are the Soviet Union and other socialist countries, the working-class movement and all anti-monopoly forces of the developed capitalist countries, as well as the national-liberation movement. The revolutionary process enjoys the peoples' sympathies, support and solidarity.

The Allende government was appreciated and generously aided by the Soviet Union, socialist Cuba, the German Democratic Republic and other socialist countries. It maintained cordial relations with most Latin American governments, fostered relations with the Andean Pact countries, signed highly useful agreements with various West European countries and established relations with Asian and African countries. Now that the peace forces are gaining influence and detente is making headway, there are more favourable conditions for the popular revolution. However, it will become impossible if concessions are made to anti-Sovietism and if it is attempted in isolation from the common stream of the progressive forces of humanity.

Chile's revolutionary forces were not disheartened by their temporary setback. They are as loyal to their fundamental views as ever. "The Communist Party," said the Party in its first statement after the coup (released in October 1973), "is absolutely convinced that its advocacy of unqualified defence of the Popular Unity government, its steps to reach understanding with other democratic forces, above all at grass roots, its effort to inspire the middle strata with confidence and direct the main blow against the principal enemies – imperialism and domestic reaction – its perseverance in strengthening the Socialist-Communist alliance and working-class unity and in promoting understanding among the Popular Unity parties, its effort to achieve greater output and higher productivity, proper financing of the enterprises in the public sector and strict labour discipline constituted an entirely correct general policy. However, this does not rule out mistakes or weaknesses in its activity."[2]

Revolutionary progress at the democratic stage, with socialism as a prospect, expresses itself in increasing interaction in the political, ideological, social and economic spheres. This can be achieved given the hegemony of the working class, which is the decisive factor for the unification of all democratic forces in a broad and solid alliance, as has already been said.

The Communist Party realised that it must uphold its independent class line in the movement for unity, a line aimed at uniting all revolutionary forces, resisting all deviations and safeguarding the future of our revolutionary process. And this means that the Party bears special responsibility for shortcomings and weak spots in pursuing that line.

The dialectics of the multiparty system and of united and firm leadership had distinctive features in Chile. There developed a broad and flexible unity implying unity of the working class itself, its alliance with other working people and understanding between it and other democratic forces. In the conditions of the revolutionary process, this unity was based on the existence of a strong and influential Communist Party, Communist-Socialist unity, which was a factor of the first importance, and an effective Popular Unity bloc comprising the Communist Party, Left Christian party, Unitary Movement for Popular Action (MAPU), MAPU-Worker Peasant Party, Radical Party, Socialist Party and Independent Popular Action.

This unity was also based on temporary agreements with other political organisations, in particular on an agreement with the Christian Democratic Party intended to assure the election of Allende to the Presidency by the entire Congress and carry out constitutional reforms relating to "democratic guarantees" and the nationalisation of the major copper mines. Besides, friendly relations were established with the Catholic Church and other churches. In October 1972, an agreement was reached under the Popular Unity Programme with the command of the armed forces, which adhered to a democratic position and support the Constitution. This found expression in the formation of a cabinet led by General Carlos Prats from November 1972 to March 1973 and in its well-known statement and its plan for establishing a public sector in the economy.

We revolutionaries cannot accomplish the revolution by ourselves but must, if we are to succeed, bring into the revolutionary process those strata that are objectively interested in the revolution but generally vacillate. Experience shows that this issue is settled in the most diverse forms. One of these forms, the multiparty system, became in Chile a means of consolidating forces in joint action, In serious political battles and in working out a common programme respecting the independence of every member of the alliance.

As the revolutionary process goes on, however, social classes and strata constantly come up against new problems and new tasks and are influenced by its laws.

Life amends programmes, especially when revolutionary activity accelerates the pace of history like a powerful locomotive. This makes it necessary for a multiparty coalition to have a sufficiently united and firm leadership capable of developing its own programme, consolidating gains and defeating reaction. Otherwise the revolution finds itself threatened. Revolutionary talk, the temptation to give priority to "competition" in recruiting forces, the stratagems of right and "left" opportunists and the formation of poles dividing the progressive camp more likely to weaken a popular government to a disastrous extent. The harsh lessons of Chile are most revealing in this respect.

However, it is obvious that the unity of the revolutionary forces has withstood the ordeal of temporary reverse. This is evidence of the solidity of the foundations of unity. Communist-Socialist unity today goes deeper than in the past; the Popular Unity coalition has arrived at better mutual understanding and the unity of all anti-fascist forces, including the Christian Democratic Party, has gained in scope through joint action. Even so, this problem and all that has happened must be analysed still more carefully if the anti-fascist struggle is to become more effective and attain its goals.

Sustained struggle

The past quarter-century has seen a substantial growth and centralisation of capital in Chile. In this period, life itself impelled the middle strata to put forward democratic demands meeting their interests and running counter to the interests of imperialism and monopoly. The formation of the Allende government was the result and culmination of a sustained struggle throughout which the domestic big bourgeoisie and imperialism endangered democratic freedoms, rights and institutions by constantly attacking them while the working class, the Communist Party and its allies campaigned for demands meeting the interests of the nation and of progress.

Due to the struggle of the working class and the people, a relatively modern democratic state was formed in Chile. In spite of the bourgeois character of this state, a struggle for power went on in it for a long time, especially between 1970 and 1973. The earlier, anti-democratic class content of the state, determined by the exploiters' interests, coexisted with democratic gains registered afterwards. The only way to consolidate these gains and set the goal of achieving socialism was to press forward the revolution and destroy the traditional anti-democratic structures. This is a problem that we think no revolution can avoid.

Some Chileans imagined that they could bypass it by uttering freedom-loving generalities or with the aid of anarchist catchwords and appeals disguising their weakness in the actual struggle against reaction. However, experience confirmed, and still confirms, that this kind of opportunism, which puts abstract things first for "bona fide" reasons while concealing concrete things in favour of momentary interests, becomes the most danger-ous variety of opportunism, which Lenin warned against. The connection between the two stages of the revolutionary process also manifests itself in the link between the respective class components. The democratic stage is characterised, in addition to a definite class composition of its motive forces, by the breadth of their alliances.

Progress towards the socialist stage does not necessarily narrow or reduce these alliances. In fact, the revolution integrates forces. He who musters more forces wins. The working class must ensure that the bloc of forces which unite to bring about revolutionary changes is stronger than the bloc backed by imperialism. Events in Chile revealed that the struggle for democracy and socialism demands unfailing vigilance, for the enemies of democracy exploit every passing superiority in strength to counterattack. This is why problems of decisive importance must be discussed and made understandable to the masses long before they become the order of the day.

Experience shows that the indecision of the middle strata could have been foreseen. It was vastly important to follow a clear-cut and firm, yet sufficiently flexible policy towards them, a principled policy that would have prevented imperialism and reaction from making the middle strata the social basis for the fascist rising. (Family ties and the social origin of most officers of the armed forces, who came from the middle strata, played a notable part in this).

Social base

The class struggle intensifies as the tasks of the democratic stage of the rev-olution are carried out, and demands concerning the advance to socialism become more emphatic. In these circumstances there is no ignoring the issue of what class is ruling society, how it succeeds in mobilising an active major-ity and how far it is able to maintain and exercise its power. The extension of the social basis of the revolutionary process in-step with its advance at the democratic phase confronts the working-class vanguard with bigger tasks and if its organisational and political growth is lagging behind the growth of the popular movement, it may find itself trailing behind events when new objective conditions mature.

The anti-monopoly and anti-imperialist democratic tasks of the revolution are accomplished depending chiefly on the solution of the contradictions of the given regime. However, every socio-economic formation is a dialectical whole complete in itself. It follows that the intricate dialectical relationship between social contradictions makes it impossible to skip stages or consider them to be very far apart.

The Chilean revolution refuted the narrow-minded concept treating all the ruling classes as the chief enemy and drawing no distinction between big landowners, rich and middle landowners, the monopoly oligarchy, diverse sections of the national bourgeoisie and the middle strata. Ultra-leftists sharing this concept accused the Chilean revolution of "reformism". It is indicative, however, that attacks of this nature were widely publicized and highlighted by the mass media, as well, which took an active part in the efforts to "destabilise" the popular government and clear the decks for the fascist coup.

Imperialism and reaction realised, of course, that the democratic, anti-imperialist, anti-monopoly and anti-latifundium revolution was paving the way for socialism. The experience of the 1970-73 period shows indeed that consistently democratic measures intertwined with rudiments of socialism. As a result of the changes carried out, the development of the Chilean economy became chiefly non-capitalist. The decisive sector of the economy stopped serving capitalist accumulation. In this situation, the process of new production objectively necessitated the replacement of the production discipline imposed by monopoly with a new discipline conditioned by the hegemony of the working class. It was necessary to establish greater worker control over production, introduce planning throughout the economy and base management on efficient functioning of the public sector and the agrarian reform sector.

We know from experience that unless we consolidate the positions we have won and are firm in carrying the revolutionary process deeper, we may risk having to retreat all along the line. Counter-revolution not only strives to prevent the transition to socialism but opposes all democratic guarantees. This is why, in self-critically analysing the Chilean events, we consider it very important to ascertain why we did not in the course of the revolutionary process take appropriate steps when objective contradictions increased, as might have been expected because this is a law of every revolution.

The fact that the formation of a popular government, the recognition of President Allende's electoral victory and the realisation of democratic changes were made possible was due to the solid unity of the working class on fundamental issues and actions, to the correct orientation of the working class and the wide range of its links of alliance, which enabled it to use organisational forms in keeping with current tasks. But subsequently the situation became even more complicated, the enemy stepped up their resistance and the working class and its allies in the democratic camp had to build up their strength.

The point is that as the revolutionary process went deeper the bourgeoisie, including those of its sections that had been hit by monopoly domination and benefited from the popular government's measures, tended more and more to proceed, above all, from the assumption that their interests were contrary to those of the working class. This tendency was also encouraged by abstract talk about the socialist future without regard to the actual tasks of the moment. However, the most negative and destructive factor was that the working class failed after all to win effective hegemony; instead, the dominant policy trend was duality and concessions, made to both right- and "left"-wing opportunists.

In April 1972, the Communist Party warned against the impending danger and, with a view to bringing about decisive progress, stressed the need to raise the role of the working class, establish a united and strict system of economic management, consolidate the gains made and isolate the more dangerous enemies. Subsequent developments showed only too plainly, however, that this line was not pursued with adequate determination. After the defeat, it was justly pointed out that "we carried on discussions and clarified our class position at the level of the leadership; but we did not encourage discussion at grass roots, among the people, sufficiently to prevent the spread of petty bourgeois. revolutionism, which injured Socialist-Communist unity and hence the revolutionary process".[3]

The split in a united and mobilising leadership became a factor for defeat. Opportunism spread in two interconnected trends. The ultra-leftists, denying the revolutionary character of the process under way, tried to impose their own notions of its development and strove, in effect, to disrupt it from within. On the other hand, the reformists overrated the peaceful aspects of the process and made a fetish of undemocratic institutions that were out of keeping with the new and more important tasks brought to the fore by life.

Paradoxically, if not unaccountably, these two varieties of opportunism constantly backed each other, being prompted by their bias against the Communists. Analysing the results of those years, we must note that the revolution succeeded in setting up democratic institutions of a new type and developing higher forms of democracy.

In some fields, it began to combine government with popular self-government. Supply and price control councils became widespread. They were led by an outstanding revolutionary, Marta Ugarte. Housing councils and mothers' committees, and production and defence committees in industry were formed. The trade unions began to assume leading functions in the social sphere. Management in industry and trade was being transformed step by step and a system of people's inspectors elected by the trade unions and supply councils was being set up. Their communal offices operated in collaboration with mass organisations. The United Workers' Centre (CUT) helped to establish its industrial belt councils.

A national economic plan for 1974 was being drafted with the participation of the masses, which became a reality in enterprises belonging to the public sector and in the agrarian-reform area. A number of treaties were signed between the Ministry of the Economy and the staffs of certain enterprises relating to the amount of output, labour productivity, raw materials supply, credit terms, wage levels, prices and investment. The working class, strongly backed by the youth and intellectuals, succeeded in maintaining order in the country during the employers' sabotage in October 1972 and August 1973.

However, no transitional situation proper was created during the revolution; that is, the revolution did not entirely achieve its democratic and anti-imperialist objectives and the opening up of the socialist perspective. This required greater democratisation and the abolition of the privileges and political power of the imperialist monopolies and the financial oligarchy. It also called for a new system of leadership in society that may be defined in scientific terms as the dictatorship of the working class and the masses of town and countryside, or people's power.

The Chilean events showed that it is very dangerous not to carry democratisation through to the end, and that it must be carried through as early as possible. This certainly implies defence of the people's democratic rights against counter-revolution by suppressing counter-revolutionary, anti-democratic activity. The Communist Party and Popular Unity realised that the power of domestic and foreign imperialist monopolies conditioned both certain basic aspects of the exercise of parliamentary authority and other, equally important, activities in industry and the military sphere. This is why Luis Corvalan insists so often that success in elections is not the most important thing in the advance of the popular forces, but only part of the complex development of a broader social struggle. Accordingly, the Party constantly warned against the danger posed by the euphoria of those who imagined that the September 1970 election had guaranteed the development of the socialist socio-economic formation.

At a time when we had won power only in part, it was essential to democratise every field of activity, to carry out far-reaching democratisation measures in economic management, extend democracy to the judiciary and the control machinery, achieve a balance of forces in favour of democracy among the military and bring the administrative; system into line with genuinely democratic standards. We stopped half-way in this respect. The Popular Unity government failed to establish effective democracy in decisive fields. Its gains, while impressive and highly noteworthy, were clearly inadequate.

Mutual understanding

Nevertheless, the tremendous headway made in this direction opened the eyes of millions of Chileans to reaction's falsehoods about the revolution. Everyone saw for himself that the revolutionary process brings the people greater freedom, assigns them a bigger public role and affords them unprecedented opportunities to raise their cultural standards while respecting the religious convictions and the customs and traditions of every population group.

All this has lost none of its importance. The position of the Church and the mutual understanding that links non-party Catholics and Christian Democrats with Popular Unity in defending human rights are based primarily on their own experience of the attitude of the government, the Communists, Socialists, Radicals and left-wing Christians towards the Christian rank and file. Besides, most Chileans discarded at a certain moment their illusions about the "independence of judicial power" and the "neutrality of the armed forces". Above all, the working class has become more conscious politically. This is seen, among other things, in its insistence on united and independent trade unions continuing to operate even amid fascist terror. The working class – and the majority of the people with it – have come to see in a state functioning in a society of class antagonisms a product of irreconcilable class contradictions.

The anti-democratic character of the decisive components of the old system of government stood out all the more when a number of democratic revolutionary changes were effected. That was when the strength of the popular government, its ability to maintain democratic changes and its activity aimed at pressing forward social changes and upholding what the people had won became particularly important. Karl Marx noted that: "In general, social reforms can never be brought about by the weakness of the strong; they must and will be called to life by the strength of the weak."[1]

The ability to defend the revolution is central to every genuinely revolutionary process, irrespective of the path it is following. The democratic phase of the revolution needs to be consolidated and carried forward, and this is inseparable from defending the revolution. Defence of the revolution must begin at the stage it has reached, for this is the only way to ensure that it moves on to the next and higher stage.

The experience of Chile points very clearly to the dialectical interlocking and interdependence of action intended to overthrow the power of the ruling classes and resist counter-revolution and action mobilising the masses to build a new society. All this took place in the course of a most complicated class struggle and social and economic changes.

The defence of revolutionary gains is neither a conspiracy nor a task of small groups isolated from the people. It is based on the popular government's desire to express the interests and aspirations of the masses, on its ability to unite the masses and mobilise them for struggle, and on its dynamic and correct creative effort. However, all this is not enough unless the masses are able to strengthen the democratic government and state as exponents of the interests of the progressive forces. It is necessary continuously to modify the system of institutions and agencies if every component of power is to function in the interests of the working class, the people and the nation.

We Chilean Communists know by experience of the damage caused to the revolution and the people by weakness in the face of reactionary violence. We have come to the conclusion that the primary duty of revolutionary forces in accomplishing the tasks of the democratic stage is to be firm in their resolve to deliver crippling blows to all who resort to counter-revolutionary violence. The effort to mobilise an active majority of the people must be supported by an appropriate mass organisation which commands all requisite means and whose members have been properly educated and trained.

To go over from the democratic to the socialist stage, the popular forces must also hold positions enabling them to take the offensive, which is not tantamount to merely widening, step by step, the range of action in the matter of expropriation or to striving to expose as many enemies as possible. It is far more important continuously to further democracy in every sphere, as I have already pointed out, strengthen the unity of the workers' militant action and raise the fighting efficiency of the Party and its allies, increase the efficiency of the popular government and isolate counter-revolutionaries.

Why did the revolutionary leadership of Chile fail in this?

I have said that there was a moment when in exercising power and mustering forces to defend its positions, everything came to depend on how resolutely and effectively the leadership pursued its policy. It was essential to exercise democratic power, to use the authority vested in the popular government. But precisely because it did not raise problems with absolute confidence, nor carry on with adequate efficiency the everyday work necessitated by these problems, the policy adopted by the leadership failed to acquire a sufficiently mobilising quality.

The Popular Unity government should have been in keeping with the given stage of its tasks in both substance and form. It was a synthesis of the authority and strength of the people. There were shortcomings in its development, and many were misled by the propaganda of reformist and anarchist concepts of power carried on by both those who praised the former system and government and those who demanded "people's rule" as the antithesis of the Popular Unity government.

Thus, the temporary defeat of the Chilean revolution confirms the dialectical connection between democratic tasks and the socialist future, as well as the dialectics of revolutionary paths, which necessitates ability and preparedness to go over from one path to another at the right moment, as the situation changes. The fascist coup of September 11, 1973, showed that the enemy remembers these objective laws at all times, even when we forget them.

NOTES

1 *Partido Comunista de Chile. Boletin del Exterior.* No. 20, 1976, p.8.
2 *Desde Chile hablan los comunistas!* Ediciones Colo-Colo, 1976, pp.28-9.
3 *Desde Chile hablan los comunistas!*, p.88.
4 Karl Marx, *The Protectionists, the Free Traders and the Working Class*, Marx and Engels Collected Works, Vol 6, p.281

Jorge Insunza

4

The Dialectic of the Roads of Revolution

Jorge Insunza

The revolutionary process in Chile was the first prolonged experiment in the peaceful development of revolution. The international Communist movement regarded it as an event whose analysis could contribute significantly to perfecting revolutionary strategy and tactics. Study of the class struggle in this period yields conclusions that enrich the theory of the development of revolution by peaceful means, clarify its limits, and underline the relevance of the Marxist-Leninist understanding of the necessity to use all forms of struggle.

For Chilean Communists, a precise assessment of the process as a whole, with an analysis of its successes and failures, is essential to the success of our efforts both now and in the future. This task, to which attention was drawn immediately after the coup, is still as important as ever.

Our experience confirms that the roads of revolution – peaceful and armed – cannot and should not be regarded as mutually exclusive. Treating them as opposite poles is dangerous to the success of the revolutionary process.

Marx, speaking for the revolutionary workers, warned the reactionaries: "We shall act against you peacefully where it is possible for us to do so, and by force of arms when that becomes necessary."[1] This definition of tactics has lost none of its significance today. A striking example of such an approach to development of the revolutionary process, when the different roads to power and its consolidation are considered in their dialectical unity, was Lenin's conception, put into practice in 1917. In April of that year, he pointed to the possibility of the peaceful development of the revolution; after the July events he spoke of the necessity of preparing for an armed uprising; in September he again considered peaceful development possible and called for efforts to realise this possibility; and finally, only a little later he drew the conclusion that there must be an armed uprising, which in fact led to the victory of October.

Our Party's interest in the problem of the peaceful development of the revolution goes back a long way. In the 1960s we made a deeper study of these problems, using the conclusions drawn from past experience to work out and creatively apply the Marxist propositions on the peaceful transition to socialism. Our notion of how this road should actually be travelled in Chile was gradually perfected on the basis of the general laws of revolution and the country's national peculiarities. The Communists proposed that the working class should become a rallying point for the majority, for all the anti-imperialist and anti-oligarchic forces, so that a government could be formed capable of effecting the revolutionary changes necessitated by the mounting crisis of Chilean society.

The aim was to carry out an anti-imperialist, anti-monopoly and agrarian revolution with the goal of advancing toward socialism. Having established two strategic stages of the revolution, we planned to put them into effect as a single unbroken, revolutionary process. This possibility rested on the objective interconnection between the goals of the two stages, and also on the leading role which the working class could and should undertake in a broad alliance with the forces interested in change. Our Party pointed out that a revolutionary crisis was looming and at the same time noted the combination of objective, subjective, national and international factors that would allow the people of Chile to gain power without the use of armed force as the chief means of struggle. This gave a powerful impetus to the development of the mass movement and greater scope for rallying the majority of the population around the working class.

Peaceful road

The Party had to explain its plans. It had to defend them from numerous attacks and overcome misunderstandings. The revolutionary character of this road was proved both in theory and practice. To avoid any misunderstandings a precise definition of the word "peaceful" was given. Peaceful development of the process did not mean that the struggle of the people's movement should proceed only within the framework of bourgeois legal forms; nor was it necessarily, let alone exclusively, to be associated with electioneering. The peaceful road (we also called it the "non-armed" road) did not, and could not, mean total repudiation of the use of violence for removing the reactionary classes from power. A revolution, as we realised, always entails violence and social coercion, although it does not always assume armed forms.

In all the documents of our Party it was noted that the choice of road did not depend only on the subjective decision of the revolutionaries. Changes in the situation should be foreseen and prepared for in advance. This idea is clearly expressed in our 1969 programme.

Whereas, previously, the stress was laid on the possibility of peaceful development of the revolution, now, as Luis Corvalan said at the 14th National Congress of the Communist Party of Chile: "The new programme declares that revolution is a complex process comprising all forms of the struggle that our people are waging, and that *its roads are determined according to the historical situation, but must invariably be based on the activity of the masses.* In view of this the revolutionary solution should not necessarily be linked in advance with any one definite road."[2]

This assessment was not associated with any change of the tactics we had adopted, but was a result of their better elaboration.

In the light of our experience it can be seen that a deeper study of the concepts of the "peaceful" and "armed" roads must be made, that they must be stripped of all ambiguity, that we must realise that they belong not to the sphere of strategy but to that of tactics, which changes according to circumstances. The political line must be analysed and checked from the standpoint of the interconnection and dialectical unity of its components. As I have noted above, our view on this point of dialectics was made more precise. But a tendency to absolutise the peaceful road still persisted. We sometimes referred to it as "the natural channel", and the correct proposition that it would be necessary at a certain stage to follow "only one line" was taken by many people as meaning that the road we were following at the given moment would be that one line.

Lenin said that a revolutionary party should be able to command all forms of struggle. He emphasised, however, that one should not confuse "fundamental recognition, in principle, of all means of struggle, of all plans and methods, provided they are expedient, with the demand at a given political moment to be guided by a strictly observed plan".[3]

When you are in the thick of the fight it is not always easy to reach a practical decision. You have to take into account what forms of struggle are dictated by the objective situation. Lenin noted this in his day and it came out very plainly in the Chilean events.

"Every form of struggle requires a corresponding technique and a corresponding apparatus," Lenin emphasised. "When objective conditions make the parliamentary struggle the principal form of struggle, the features of the apparatus for parliamentary struggle inevitably become more marked in the Party."[4] Intensification of such features is dangerous in the sense that it can hamper the skilful change of tactics that the situation demands, and this danger can be diminished only by very attentive and thoughtful action by the leadership and the whole Party. We were thoughtful and attentive, but this was not enough.

Despite some oversights, the basic theoretical propositions of a strategic and partially tactical character evolved by the Party helped to mobilise the broad masses in the fight for revolutionary goals. The conditions that brought the developing revolutionary situation to a head were created mainly by unarmed means. Practice showed that a political line which correctly defined the main enemies and the direction of the main blow, put the main emphasis on development of the mass struggle, and was geared to the pre-election situation, could lead to victory. Following this line through stubborn class battles in all spheres of social activity enabled the Popular Unity alliance to win the post of President of the Republic. The victory of 1970 gave the revolutionary government access to power (or rather partial power) with the help of the bourgeois electoral machinery and the laws of bourgeois democracy. Lenin's theory of revolution thus became reality.

Does this mean that the reverses that followed prove the impossibility of carrying out a revolution by peaceful means (as the ideologues of the big and petty bourgeoisie are now saying)? A genuinely scientific analysis certainly does not warrant this conclusion. At the same time, in analysing the situation we see what steps should have been taken but were not taken or not taken energetically and resolutely enough to exploit the advantages already gained by peaceful means.

The following general conclusion may also be drawn. The peaceful development of revolution is a process that is completed only when the question of power is finally decided, when the possibility of restoration of the power of the old classes has been ruled out, and the new democracy and new leadership of society have been firmly established. Certain phases can be defined in this process. The popular forces' winning of power (at first only partial power) completes the first phase. Then comes the period of solving the "second-day" problems – the assertion of the revolutionary gains and the consolidation of forces, when the question on the agenda is "Who will win?" The general preconditions for victory in both phases exist, but the pressure on the revolutionary movement in each differs. And reaction may be so fierce that it imposes the need for use of revolutionary armed force. This means that the revolutionary process in the second phase must follow a different course from what it did in the first. But, on the one hand, this does not cancel the first step, the first victory and, on the other, reaction's chances of provoking civil war are diminished if the revolutionaries do their work well.

The experience of Chile up to 1970 and for a certain time afterwards suggests that the peaceful development of the revolutionary process is the most acceptable road, if there is the opportunity and, of course, only while that opportunity exists. In a revolutionary situation only the absence of conditions for the peaceful development of the revolution or their having been whittled down, makes it possible and imperative to take the road of armed struggle.

The possibilities of developing the revolution by peaceful means in present-day conditions are closely linked with the substantial changes that have taken place in the world since the victory of the Great October Socialist Revolution. The growing prestige of the socialist countries makes these possibilities more and more realistic. It is becoming increasingly difficult for imperialism to export counter-revolution, to engage in direct armed intervention that has to be answered by the use of armed revolutionary force.

The victory of the Vietnamese revolution, which struck a serious blow at the export of counter-revolution, is a symbol of our times. This is also true of the victory in Cuba, which showed, apart from anything else, that these are situations in which imperialism cannot intervene successfully with its own forces. And although both revolutions involved a fierce armed struggle, they nevertheless confirm that the existence of international preconditions offer revolution a peaceful road in cases where the international factors combine with the national.

The Chilean events also reaffirmed the fact that the influence of international factors depends largely on the position taken by the political leaders of the revolutionary process, on their ability to use these factors as a lever, on their attitude to the support that the socialist countries are quite prepared to offer the progressive movement without any strings attached.

Some groups stress the difficulties of the peaceful transition arising from the domination of imperialism in Latin America. They focus attention on the ferocity with which imperialism defends its "strategic reserve". To this they add the argument that geographical position is a factor of political significance. Here we are certainly dealing with real facts, but they can be compensated, and more than compensated, if the revolutionary movements are firmly oriented on support from the forces of existing socialism and proletarian solidarity. This is an extremely important question of principle and practice. It is not isolation from the socialist countries but, on the contrary, strengthening of ties with them that improves the chances of success on the peaceful road, or, come to that, any success at all for the revolution, no matter which road it takes.

International solidarity

The new international situation is one of the main justifications for the general assertion that today peaceful revolution stands a better chance. However, the improvement of the balance of world forces does not imply the conclusion that this road must always be followed in all circumstances. The real possibilities of success on this road, possibilities that in the past were regarded as extremely thin, are now somewhat better.

On the other hand, the Chilean experience shows that imperialism has adapted its tactics to the new world conditions and evolved a practical alternative to direct armed intervention as a means of terminating the revolutionary process. We have in mind action in the sphere of economics, international relations, ideology, the armed forces, and so on. Chile offers a wealth of material for studying these methods. Their detailed analysis is beyond the scope of this article, but it should be noted that the success the revolutionaries have in combating these methods is linked with the question of their close cooperation with the socialist countries, their reliance on international solidarity – which was something that we did not have enough of.

Given a close interlocking of international and national factors, the key to the success of the revolutionary process undoubtedly lies with the internal factors. In Chilean conditions the revolution was based on the winning of a solid majority united around the working class.

As we know, the victory at the 1970 elections that made it possible to form the Popular Unity government had the support not of an absolute majority, but of only 36% of the voters. The government took up its duties after an intense class struggle that lasted for two months. During this struggle the Popular Unity alliance was able to thwart imperialism's first secret operation, which ended in an unsuccessful attempt at a coup d'état.[5] Popular Unity won over the majority of the public and forced the class enemy on to the defensive.

Without this, there would have been no respect for the results of the elections and the struggle for power could not have been won.

So, we have a factual basis for regarding the victory in the elections as a step that was of great importance but was not a sufficient guarantee that the oligarchy and imperialism, which still had dominant positions in society, would respect the expression of the people's will. We believe that the gains of Popular Unity were determined not just by the victory in the elections, but by the struggle before and after the elections.

Whereas the basic condition for the initial victory was the creation of a tested and effective majority for the achievement of immediate goals, the decisive condition for completion of the process was expansion of this majority, its consolidation and activation. Action should have been taken to shift the unstable, indecisive balance of forces in favour of the people and make it decisive.

Use should have been made of the positions of power already gained, and the required government measures should have been carried out from these positions. This was an essential condition for consolidation of real people's power, for the victorious completion of the democratic revolution and a swift transition to the socialist revolution. This was the main condition for achieving revolutionary goals by peaceful means, for preventing reactionary violence.

Undoubtedly, the key problem, as we have already noted, was to achieve monolithic working-class unity and gather round it, under its leadership, a strong alliance of the intermediate sections of the population, above all the peasants, and also the broad middle strata of the urban population, which in Chile have considerable social weight, while at the same time winning over, or at least neutralising, sections of the national bourgeoisie.

The intermediate strata, as we know, are between two poles, the revolutionary and counter-revolutionary, and have a tendency – first, economic, then political and ideological – to waver between these poles. The counter-revolutionary pole of Chilean society is represented by the financial and land-owning oligarchies and imperialism, and to ensure victory the working class had to do everything possible to isolate them. It had a very wide circle of essential and possible allies. But this opportunity was not used to the full. On the contrary, as the revolution proceeded the working class became noticeably isolated, particularly at the time of the coup, and this isolation was, in fact, the chief factor in its defeat. Not that the working class failed to acquire powerful allies, but it fell far short of taking in a wide enough circle to secure its victory.

Formidable battles were fought over this crucial question in the three years of the Popular Unity government's activity. The leftist elements played an extremely negative role from the standpoint of working-class interests. Their incorrect actions, which came from mistaken notions of the character of the Chilean revolution and were widely exploited by imperialism and the reactionaries, aroused first anxiety and then panic among the broad intermediate strata.

Obviously, one can win over the majority of the people only when tasks are set that have really become relevant to the given stage of the revolution and the given political situation. This means finding the key to each stage and taking a responsible stand on the conclusions drawn. At the same time, the working class can become a focus of unity and spread its influence to the intermediate strata if, in conducting its general political line, it is able to undertake the defence not only of its own interests but also the essential interests of these social strata and develop its own revolutionary momentum. These are the principles on which government policy and the forces of Popular Unity should have worked to win over allies, consolidate the alliance and at the same time prevent reaction from influencing the strata that both sides wanted to win over.

Analysing events from this standpoint we can see that along with considerable, truly historic achievements, such as nationalisation of the major copper mines, agrarian reform, creation of a state-owned sector in the economy there were also clear weaknesses in the Chilean revolutionary process. A host of complex problems had to be dealt with in the unusual situation created by the imperialist economic blockade. This meant that even the revolutionary changes that had been carried through could not be exploited to the extent that circumstances required.

Winning the majority
The disunity in the leadership of the political alliance led to right and "left" deviations. There were failures in the drive for real democracy that should have united those forces that had an objective interest in change. Reactionary schemes were not always countered. On the contrary, they were actively promoted by the press, most of which was under reactionary control, and with the help of the press the government and the popular movement were attacked with a viciousness unusual in Chile. All these factors hindered consolidation of the majority.

But winning over the majority was not enough. The power of the majority had to be used to gain the upper hand over the enemy in all spheres. As Lenin wrote: "... in time of revolution it is not enough to ascertain the 'will of the majority' – you must *prove to be stronger* at the decisive moment and in the decisive place; you must win".[6] The revolution must be able to defend itself. The main weapon in this defence is the new state that the revolution must create. In the context of peaceful transition, this gives rise to some very complex problems, which again reveal the dialectical unity of the possible roads of revolution.

The development of the Chilean revolutionary process along the peaceful road, as has already been noted gave the popular movement partial power. This success proved, on the one hand, the strength of the popular movement and, on the other, its inability at that moment to win full state power.

There is no reason to believe that such a situation is bound to repeat itself in any revolution developing on peaceful lines. In principle, it is possible "on the very first day" to capture all the commanding heights or at least all the civil authorities in the government apparatus (executive and legislative). But this will still be the old state apparatus and in all probability there will be within it and almost surely outside it organs of power that are not controlled by the revolution. The whole apparatus, as experience has shown, will be highly reluctant to carry out transformations and apply the coercion that is needed in such cases, until substantial changes have been made in its content and form. The decisive factor is the deep-going democratisation of the state apparatus, the creation of mechanisms instituting genuine popular control over the functioning of the state, and transfer of as many as possible of its powers to the masses. The positive experience gained in this field, for example, in the control of supply, the distribution and pricing of staple goods, offers a convincing picture of the possibilities in this sphere. Control "from below", from the masses, allows them to realise their power in practice and promote essential changes in the state apparatus from outside, changes that are effected with the assistance of the revolutionary leadership from within.

Democratic gains

One of the aspects of this problem is connected with observance of bourgeois legality, which made it possible to win power. This problem loomed particularly large in Chile precisely because the popular movement had won only executive power, while its adversaries had retained strong positions in other organs of state power: parliament, the judiciary, the inspectorates, and so on. This unique situation created barriers to the passage of the new laws that were needed to consolidate real democratisation and revolutionary reforms.

On the basis of our own experience, however, we can draw the conclusion that, thanks to the democratic gains that were achieved by the working class and the people in the course of the whole preceding struggle and that are one of the major factors in ensuring the peaceful development of the revolution, the revolutionaries can by working from their position in the state bodies make very effective use of existing legislation. The use of the legal machinery must, of course, be combined with active campaigning on the part of the masses. Nationalisation of the big monopolies proved the existence of such possibilities.

When all this has been said, however, our experience indicates that the struggle of the masses, even under a popular government, cannot be restricted to the very narrow limits of the previous legislation because there is no room within this framework for all the revolutionary activity that is needed.

This leads us to the conclusion that there must be a unitary organisation embodying the people's power that has been generated "from below". Attempts to solve this problem were begun more or less spontaneously in Chile. From the experiment in setting up councils on supply and prices we moved on to setting up other bodies bringing together representatives of the masses. But this process did not culminate in the formation of new organs of state power. At the same time we do not hold that some special organisation has to be set up. In many countries, probably, one of the existing organisations could become the required organ of state power.

As Lenin observed in his day: "The proletariat has approached, and will approach this singular task in different ways." Analysing the actual situation at the time, he went on: "In some parts of Russia the February-March Revolution puts nearly complete power in its hands. In others the proletariat may, perhaps, in a 'usurpatory' manner, begin to form and develop a proletarian militia. In still others, it will probably strive for immediate elections of urban and rural local government bodies on the basis of universal, etc, suffrage, in order to turn them into revolutionary centres."[7]

The main thing, then, is to see to it that people can express their will and effectively exercise power "from below", that they take a direct part in building the new democracy. Without this the "power at the top" cannot carry out its revolutionary tasks in the face of the embittered opposition of the reactionaries.

In Chile mistakes were made in this respect. There was not enough clarity and unity among the revolutionaries regarding the type of state that had to be created, or the form and content of democracy. This vagueness led to hesitations that were expressed both in repudiation of the need for any dictatorship (which inevitably weakened the campaign for transformation of the bourgeois state), and in the urge to immediately set up proletarian dictatorship, for which at that moment the right conditions were lacking, and which would have meant a leap into a vacuum and would have led to the isolation of the working class. This lack of clarity created a kind of anarchy, because weakness in revolutionary theory means weakness of the subjective factor, of any guiding influence upon the efforts of the masses to strengthen the people's government.

The successful completion of any revolutionary path is bound to entail solving the specific problem of building up a favourable balance of armed forces. The elements of tactics evolved by Marx, Engels and Lenin are well known. We have in mind their statements referring mainly to the road of armed struggle. Without going into a detailed analysis, however, it can be said that all these elements should also be taken into account in evolving a conception of the revolution on peaceful lines. This kind of development does not presuppose an armed uprising or civil war, but care must be taken to achieve a balance of forces favourable to the revolution, and precisely for the purpose of preventing the reactionaries from unleashing armed conflict.

It is clear that one of the crucial factors is the situation in the armed forces and the forces for maintaining public order. How did we in Chile approach this problem?

During the first stage, right up to its victorious conclusion in 1970, we tried to arrange matters so that the armed forces would not act against the popular movement, and thus to create conditions in which a reactionary putsch would be impossible. In doing so we relied on the tradition that the armed forces did not interfere in party politics (a line they had more or less observed for about 40 years), and on the forces within the army that were loyal to the constitution and were oriented towards recognition of the popular victory achieved at the polls.

We stressed the fact that the Chilean armed forces were not directly connected with the big monopolies, that the officers came mainly from the middle strata, who had themselves experienced the effects of the crisis, that the junior officers, NCOs and rank and file came from the working class or the peasantry, from the poorest sections of the population. We said that the armed forces could not therefore remain indifferent to the process of transformation.

At the same time we pointed out that the deepening of the crisis created a new situation. "It has become a reality, for instance, that the armed forces are a new factor in national politics. It may be said that the period of the non-participation of the armed forces in political life, a non-participation that was never absolute, has ended or is nearing its end."[8]

Corvalan added: "Of course, one must take into account the conditions in which the armed forces were built up, and particularly the fact that in the recent decades their professional training has experienced the influence of the Pentagon."[9]

It may, I think, be asserted that the basic orientation on securing first and foremost non-interference by the armed forces, what we called their "neutralisation", was correct, just as it was correct for us to base ourselves on certain existing democratic traditions and consideration of the class composition of the armed forces. We see clearly now, however, that this was totally insufficient, in addition to which our policy in this field was based on certain theoretically unfounded assumptions.

For example, we regarded the armed forces' "professionalism" as something valuable, something on which one could rely in trying to prevent antipopular action. In reality, this feature does nothing whatever to strengthen progressive positions in the armed forces. On the contrary, it tends to make them even more isolated from the people and their problems. Its encouragement creates a habit of mind that puts professionalism above everything else and takes the place of the class attitudes that are determined by the soldier's social origin.

The Chilean experience has shown that: while "neutralisation" was necessary and sufficient as a first step, for getting the Popular Unity government into power, the completion of the revolutionary process makes demands of a different order. Neutralisation is a passing phase. It cannot by its very nature be anything else. As time goes on, the contradiction is bound to be resolved in one direction or another – for revolution or for counter-revolution. So, in the course of the process a solution must be found to the question of winning the armed forces over to the people's side by thoroughly democratising them, and this can only be done as a result of a very bitter confrontation on all fronts.

Here the dialectic that Marx discovered between revolution and counter-revolution is revealed to the full. The demands upon the revolution increase as it goes ahead, because the revolution must go on right up to the point when it becomes irreversible, and as it consolidates its positions it evokes increasingly furious opposition from the counter-revolutionary forces. Consequently, things that sufficed during the first stages do not suffice later on.

Experience shows that persistent efforts must be made to transform the armed forces, using all acceptable means. The chief method, we repeat, is thorough democratisation with the help of the growing influence exerted on the armed forces by the working class and the people. Certain steps were taken in this direction. To some extent the process of drawing the military into the drive to transform the country was achieved, and this helped to bring them into closer contact with the people and give them an understanding of the people's problems. Some patriotically-minded regular servicemen gave a good account of themselves in the state apparatus: in the complex situation in October 1972, for example, during the counter-revolutionary attempt, it was the alliance of the popular movement with the patriotic sections of the armed forces that ensured the people's victory. Moreover, it must be admitted that the shortcomings in this field were not caused by any constitutional restrictions, but were due to the political failings of the revolutionary forces. Here too, the left-sectarian element played a negative role.

During that period we stated: "The military establishment too, needs change, but that change should not be imposed on it. It must be initiated by the military, as a matter of their own conviction." This assertion obviously does not take into account all aspects of the problem. To achieve change, it is not enough to take action within the army alone. There must also be a struggle for the armed forces coming from outside. It must be waged by suitable means both in the context of armed revolutionary struggle and in the context of peaceful revolutionary development. As the Vietnamese military strategist, Vo Nguyen Giap, said, the essence of the law of revolutionary force lies in the combination of political forces with armed forces. This is applicable to any revolutionary road.

Military balance
As already noted, we did achieve some successes on this road. But we did not do all that we needed to do or all that we could have done. We did not succeed in winning over the army to the people's side, or in ensuring a favourable balance of military forces in other respects. And when the balance of political forces was upset this led to a crisis.

If we consider only the result of our experience, it may be asserted, as some people do, that we are discussing an insoluble problem, that an armed conflict is always inevitable. On the other hand, if we examine the development of our revolution as a whole, the conclusion is different. The problem can be solved in conditions when the revolutionary process is following a basically peaceful path. The better the revolutionary movement is prepared to defend its gains in all fields, the more likely it is to be solved.

The Chilean revolution has suffered a temporary defeat. This does not mean, however, that there is nothing left of the successes achieved thanks to the people's government, that great historic creation of our people. The efforts of reaction to deny them have yielded no results. The contrast between past and present is so striking that many of those who only yesterday stood aloof from the popular movement, or even acted against it, are today becoming ever more convinced of the need for unity with that movement. The critical analysis of the Chilean events and fair assessment of the great advances made by the masses in that period also encourage unity. The Party's policy is maturing on the basis of a profound assimilation of the lessons of the past, which will enable it to overcome present difficulties and in the near future confidently blaze the trail for further struggle.

Notes

1 Karl Marx, *Political action and the working class*. Speech by Marx at the London Conference of the International, September, 1871.
www.marxists.org/archive/marx/works/1871/09/politics-speech.htm
2 Luis Corvalán, *Camino de Victoria*. Santiago de Chile, septiembre de 1971, pág.331.
3 Lenin, *What is to be Done?* Collected Works, Vol. 5, p.391
4 Lenin, *The Crisis of Menshevism,* Collected Works, Vol. 11, p.354.
5 A reference to the murder of General Rene Schneider by far-right military forces.
6 Lenin, *Constitutional Illusions*, Collected Works, Vol. 25, p203. Progress Publishers, Moscow, 1964.
7 Lenin, *Letters from Afar,* Collected Works, Vol. 23, p331
8 Corvalán, *Camino de Victoria*, p.315.
9 Ibid., p.425.

Gladys Marin: leader of the Communist Youth of Chile, 1972

5

The Working Class and its Policy of Alliances

Gladys Marin

The assumption of power in Chile by the Popular Unity government was neither a chance development, nor a product of miscalculation on the part of reaction, as some believed. It was a victory resulting from united action by the people in which the working class played the leading role, from a decades-long struggle that surged high in the 1950s and 1960s.

That was when the Socialist-Communist alliance grew stronger and the United Workers' Centre (CUT) was formed under whose leadership big strikes for both economic and political demands took place. The peasants fought in an organised fashion for land and townspeople for housing; there developed a vast and powerful movement of students and academic personnel for university reform. Using new forms, young people joined with a boldness typical of their age in a struggle whose objectives were determined by the need for revolutionary change. Characteristically, political freedoms were extended in those years, life in the country was democratised and the people gained in political maturity. Their political awareness was shaped in large measure by the political struggle when, during the 1958 and 1964 election campaigns, they backed Salvador Allende's nomination for the presidency.

Our Party's correct policy under Christian Democratic rule – a policy of uniting all progressives and democrats among the opposition forces, in the government, and of resisting all reactionaries in both the government and the opposition – enabled us to bring it home to the masses that the Christian Democratic government's promises of reform were illusory, and to call their attention to pressing political and social problems.

These problems, which agitated the most diverse population groups, were recovery of Chile's natural resources, primarily the major copper mines, a reform of property rights, ending the latifundium agricultural system through a far-reaching agrarian reform, creating new jobs, ending backwardness, and taking steps to assure the country's development as an independent and sovereign state.

The conviction that Chile needed deep-going economic, social and political changes became ultimately part of the social consciousness of most Chileans. It found reflection in the policy of the parties that subsequently joined Popular Unity and in the sentiments of most Christian Democrats and independents.

It was in that turbulent atmosphere that late in 1969 the Popular Unity bloc came into existence. Its programme was in keeping with the interests of the majority of the population and called for profound changes in Chilean society.

Popular Unity was established due chiefly to the Communists. The Party had a meaningful political programme and made a correct assessment of the situation, indicating who were the principal enemies and inferring that a broad alliance of progressive forces was needed to isolate reaction.

The Socialist and Radical parties and the Christian Democrats who had withdrawn from their party to form the MAPU (Movement for United Popular Action) party made a decisive contribution to the formation of Popular Unity.

Revolutionary alliance

The victory on September 4, 1970, was achieved primarily by the working class and the more advanced peasants in alliance with the revolutionary forces of the urban petty bourgeoisie and a sizeable part of the middle strata. To make further headway, it was necessary to strengthen the alliance by increasing the leading role of the working class and reinforcing it with allies from new population groups.

Our policy of alliance was based on an in-depth study of realities. Imperialist domination and the existence of a monopolistic and landed oligarchy whose interests run counter to those of the immense majority of the population were at the root of the main contradictions that had to be resolved in Chile. The working class needed to come to terms with all social strata whose interests were affected by the domination of imperialism and the domestic oligarchy or a least to neutralise this or that stratum.

The popular forces had a certain experience that could help them attain this goal. It grew noticeably due to the alliance which diverse ideological currents – Marxist, Christian and Rationalist – formed in electing Allende President. The alliance developed fast as the result of a continuous search for common ground, with emphasis on what made for unity in the struggle against the common enemy and fostered the people's militancy. About 15,000 branch committees were formed during the election campaign. They constituted a political contingent possessing a huge potential for effecting revolutionary changes.

In these circumstances, it was necessary to press forward with invariable regard to Lenin's statement that "the more powerful enemy can be vanquished only by exerting the utmost effort, and by the most thorough, careful attentive, skilful and obligatory use of any, even the smallest, rift between the enemies and also by taking advantage of any, even the smallest, opportunity of winning a mass ally, even though this ally is temporary, vacillating, unstable, unreliable and conditional".[1]

To carry on a common policy making the working class the pivot and driving force of revolutionary change, it was essential to strengthen the unity of the working class itself and then that of all wage workers, which, in turn, had to contribute to the formation of a broad national alliance of popular forces around the working class. Politically, it was based on Socialist-Communist unity of action. Trade union unity was promoted by the formation of CUT. The revolutionary forces' strong influence on the working people was demonstrated when, in 1972, CUT was founded and its leadership elected by direct vote. Large groups of voters (32.5% and 26%, respectively) backed Communist and Socialist trade unionists; the Radicals and MAPU were also represented.

On the other hand, the vote showed that the Christian Democratic Party (CDP) was still influential among the working people (it polled 25.9% of the votes) and that, while organising work was greatly intensified, large numbers of wage and salary earners were still unorganised. Then there were the many small industrial enterprises and handicraft workshops, employing 39% of the industrial work-force, according to statistics for 1967 and 1968. There was also the fast growth of the proportion of wage workers due to an influx of labour from other social classes and strata, chiefly from the peasantry, as well as to an influx of young people only just beginning their working lives. The national work-force increased by 16% in a mere five years (1966-71). Both these realities called for a consolidation of forces in the trade union movement and for sustained effort to enlighten socially those who joined the ranks of the working class.

In that process of change, it was no easy task to win over the majority of working people. Many mistakes were made. Take the economic sphere, for example. Miscalculations in Popular Unity policy bred, in particular, a trend towards wasteful spending out of proportion with the country's possibilities. The policy of fixed prices came up against excessive economic demands which conflicted with the programme for wage increases envisaged by the Popular Unity government and the trade unions. Whereas the 1971 plan provided for a 40% increase (which exceeded the price growth), the actual increase averaged more than 50%. Contrary to the policy framed by the government, many enterprises put up wages by 100%, 200% or even 500% over and above plan indices. Reaction seized on these blunders to pursue its destabilisation policy, as was only to be expected. Even those who had always opposed the working people's demands now eagerly supported the most unreasonable demands.

Of course, a further drawback was that certain trade union quarters supporting the government failed to realise that the situation had changed. They stuck to slogans of the past calling for economic strikes. They took advantage of the attention which the new national leadership gave to the working people's needs, as well as of the loosening of the employers' arbitrary methods.

Experience shows that the demand for better economic conditions, and other specific demands, which are generally an expression of the working people's struggle against the ruling classes can be used by these classes for their own ends if the working people lose sight of the overall situation during the formation of a popular government.

The Chilean events also show that right- and "left"-wing opportunism can, objectively, converge in such circumstances. This is not accidental, we believe, but very typical and likely to recur at critical junctures. Competition between ultra-leftist and rightist trends in and outside the working class for the formulation of extreme slogans was added proof of the need to combat opportunism.

Our experience indicates that such a fight, far from weakening the working people's unity of action and cohesion, is a requisite of their unity and helps those influenced by opportunists join in the united movement. The conspirators' plans for a coup invariably provided for the use of opportunism and it was used, in particular, for backing the employers' strikes in October 1972 and July-August 1973.

Opportunist trends were based on the factors we have mentioned: the very composition of Chile's work-force, the existence of disorganised and apolitical groups in this structure and the influx of a new workforce with an ideology of its own. In addition, the revolutionary forces made mistakes in their activity among the working people. Right-wing opportunism and ultra-leftism had a certain mass backing which, though not very large, was fairly strong.

To carry forward the revolutionary process, it was indispensable, along with the ideological struggle against influences alien to the working class, to enlist the working people's widest participation in economic management, in government, in the activity of every social sector. Accordingly, our Party repeatedly raised the issue of working-class policy in the course of Chile's economic transformation. I think it is important to give an idea of the Party's actual approach to this matter.

"The battle for production is no battle unless there are specific plans, precise objectives and genuine participation by the working people. When speaking of plans, we mean neither tentative calculations, nor the formulation of forecasts in terms customary under capitalism. We put forward plans setting definite tasks and containing estimates in regard to production, marketing, investment, finance, the work-force, labour productivity, average wages, exports and imports, social and cultural measures, and the use of surpluses. Without such plans, we cannot achieve the stability needed to raise productivity and ensure that enterprises in the public sector operate at a profit.

"The formulation and fulfilment of these plans must not be seen as something bureaucratic. They should constitute a process in which guidelines prepared according to scientific criteria provide the basis for decision-making, with the widest participation of the working people. The plans should specify monthly section assignments, so that every worker and every technician may understand them and ensure fulfilment. Managing boards should report to general workers' meetings monthly on progress in carrying out plans. Instead of employer tyranny and workers handing in demands, the way must be paved in the public and mixed sectors for democratic agreements on production plans and wages, to be drafted in cooperation with the trade unions as exponents of the will of the working class in its new role of leading force of the country invested with revolutionary and patriotic responsibilities."[2]

Our policy was not merely formulated in general terms. Much was done to put it into practice. Unquestionable gains were registered, for instance, at the Yarur, Textil Progreso, Madeco, Socora, Inmoar and other enterprises which were managed efficiently in accordance with the government's general guidelines, and where worker participation in management had become a reality. This contributed to better organisation, operation and bigger profits. Also worthy of note are the efforts made for the organisation of machine tools, production planning, material incentives, and planned use of foreign exchange in the public and mixed sectors.

The steps taken by the Allende government in this field were of historic significance if viewed against the background of the Chilean situation of the time. From today's point of view, however, they were much too limited.

Social consciousness

The government succeeded in bringing the working people into management in many enterprises. New distribution channels were created and the trade unions had a say in major national problems. This was important to the nation's progress and helped foster the working people's social consciousness and introduce new forms of labour discipline replacing discipline based on capitalist exploitation. The government was successful above all where the workers had assumed greater responsibility for management. But where they had not done so the government came up against manifestations of anarchy that harmed production and, more dangerous still, lowered government prestige.

This prevented the use for the people's good of the advantages of the early structural changes effected in the country. The introduction of new forms of worker participation in management outside the trade unions likewise had a negative effect, for it delayed the workers' actual involvement in management and led to the wrong notion that the unions should have nothing to do with management and should confine their role to making economic demands.

However along with trends reducing worker participation in management there developed many other trends which contributed to worker unity and vigilance. The conclusion, proved correct by revolutionary practice, that these changes are likely to rapidly raise the people's social consciousness has been confirmed by the Chilean experience. The working class played the decisive role in situations that were very difficult for the government. During the October 1972 employers' strike aimed at paralysing industry, the workers took over and resumed production shortly after. The revolutionary movement had new opportunities in spite of difficulties. The facts satisfied the workers that they were equal to managing the enterprises by themselves.

It is indicative that the formation of the public sector was a result of major actions by labour. However, in some cases, when the government decided to transfer an enterprise to the public sector, it could not do so, usually because it could not reach agreement with the workers. Worker participation in management took more clear-cut forms in the nationalised enterprises. As for the private sector no suitable forms of participation were found even though there too the workers set up committee-like bodies to supervise production and ensure that the employers did not act contrary to the national interest.

The paramount requisite of success was mutual understanding between the Socialists and Communists and joint action by Popular Unity. But the lack of a united leadership tended to reduce the workers' revolutionary strength and left room for the spread of alien tendencies in the working-class movement. To perform its role as the centre of the unity being formed and as the motive power of revolutionary change, the working class had to express and uphold both its own interests and those of the classes and strata it needed to unite around itself.

Peasant influence

The primary task was to strengthen the worker-peasant alliance since it was not strong enough as yet, even though in the 1960s the rural population had become more organised and the struggle in the countryside was on the rise. The changes that had occurred were very considerable. The number of agricultural workers' strikes increased from three in 1960 to 39 in 1964, 693 in 1967 and 1,580 in 1970. After the agrarian reform law had been passed, the more advanced sections of the rural population realised that the depth of the process would depend on the scope of their activity. In 1970, 368 farm estates went to those who worked on them, chiefly as a result of the struggle for the agrarian reform.

An equally significant change came about in the organisation of the rural population. The membership of peasant trade union confederations went up from 103,664 in 1969 to 277,895 in 1972; growth was more marked in organisations led by Communists or Socialists. As a result, Popular Unity, above all the Communists, won greater influence in rural areas during the 1973 general election.

The worker-peasant alliance undoubtedly grew much stronger under Popular Unity rule (as well as under the Frei administration, which initiated an agrarian reform). At the same time, more rural inhabitants were involved in national affairs. The government, first of all the Communists, took numerous measures to aid the countryside, especially in 1973. The campaign for the full implementation of the agrarian reform, directed above all against the latifundium holders, was highly important because its results had their effect on the entire process of democratic development. The latifundia were a barrier to the development of agriculture and to the country's overall progress.

But while far-reaching gains were made whose effect is bound to show in the future, the popular government's rural policy was not exempt from miscalculations. The government did not cater to all the rural groups listed in

its programme. The agrarian reform benefited chiefly the agricultural workers and semi-proletarians. This was an achievement but it was not enough.
The beneficiaries should have included the small peasants and those of the
semi-proletarians who had somewhat bigger plots. Account should have been
taken of the interests of all strata that could have derived definite benefits
from the popular government's policy and rallied in its support as a result.

"There are over 200,000 holdings that are smaller than the established
40-hectare plots," said Luis Corvalan in his report to the Central Committee, which met in August 1972 to discuss the agrarian question, "on which
hundreds of thousands of Chileans work. We cannot supply the country if
we renounce their output. The popular government has extended its aid to
them in credits but this is not enough. It is necessary to help them organise in
cooperatives, grant them more credits, effectively increase government pur-
chases of farm produce and, above all, guarantee in reality the security of
land tenure.

"Small and medium farmers should become allies of the historic process
going on in Chile. Anyone whose clumsy approach pushes them towards the
other side is a counter-revolutionary."[3]

The results we can now sum up show that those shortcomings were by
no means fully removed. The situation was aggravated by the fact that many
proprietors felt increasingly uncertain owing to actions provoked by ultra-
leftists with the aim of seizing lands which did not come under the agrarian
reform, and reaction used this in its propaganda.

The government did not always counter such actions properly.

It was also unfortunate both politically and economically that in carrying
out the agrarian reform the authorities often ignored the peasants' opinion
and tried to impose organisational forms from above, skipping certain stages
of the process of establishing agricultural cooperatives. In August 1972 the
Communist Party spelled out the state of affairs.

"We can draw some conclusions from the experience gained in this field,"
it stated. "Neither do the *asentamientos* [farm co-operatives] set up by the
Christian Democrats, nor the agrarian reform centres set up under the present government entirely satisfy the peasants. We consider that the fundamental task brooking no delay is to revise all these organisational forms and
take account of the peasants' opinion and interests without fail, for this is the
only way to win their support in carrying out the big tasks facing us in the
countryside."[4]

This was one of the problems that was not solved properly. Another short-
coming was that in searching for new forms of organising production and
property, attention was focused entirely on the sector in which the agrarian
reform had been carried out. No serious attempts were made to encourage
the development of cooperative forms of land tenure by small proprietors as
envisaged by the fundamental programme of the Popular Unity government.

The ultra-leftists exploited these miscalculations. Some of their moves
were a reflection of the real problems of diverse segments of the rural population but the solutions they offered were wrong.

The "land hunger" affecting a substantial part of the rural population requires new forms of carrying out the agrarian reform with due regard to the interests of all social strata.

In Chile, as in some other Latin American countries, achieving mutual understanding with the urban middle strata was a matter of growing importance for the working-class policy of alliance. The numerical strength of these strata and, more important, their increasing political leverage played a role.

The urban population was growing at the expense of the rural. In 1970 the economically active rural population added up to a mere 23.9%. Numerically, the middle strata are second only to the working class (in relation to the population as a whole). Theirs is a very heterogeneous composition, for some of them have taken shape as a result of the preservation of pre-capitalist production forms, while others have developed under the capitalist mode of production.

In 1968, as much as 94% of Chile's industry consisted of handicraft workshops and small factories employing up to 49 workers each. This section of the middle strata – the handicraftsmen and some of the small manufacturers were exploited by monopoly groups and the financial oligarchy. The changes effected by the Popular Unity government delivered them from exploitation, which meant that they ought to have welcomed or at least taken a neutral stand on' them. All the early measures for structural changes were carried out at a time when the balance of forces was favourable. To consolidate this situation, it was essential not only to turn the developing public sector into the most dynamic economic sector but to establish relations of a new type with private enterprises, with which every enterprise in the public sector was already linked, especially when many of the latter group became dependent on the former for raw materials.

Small and medium manufacturers increased their profits but they did not consider this a result of the changes brought about in the country. Indeed, many of them turned out to be involved in profiteering and black-market deals (these developments were spurred by reaction's destabilisation policy). They regarded the restrictive measures adopted against these practices as proof of "curbs" on their activity.

The Chilean experience has confirmed Lenin's thought that these strata vacillate between a desire to cast off the fetters of big capital and a dread of revolutionary change. In spite of the opportunities afforded them for growth and activity, Chile's revolutionary forces failed to demonstrate that the progress made was a result of the changes being carried out. They failed to establish solid relations of a new type between the state, the public sector and private enterprises. The lack of mutual understanding was also due to excesses in setting up the public sector. A sizeable part of the petty bourgeoisie and many handicraftsmen joined in the employers' strikes, being misled by reaction's demagogical slogan of "defending property" and the demand for "freedoms" whereas the real aim of those who provoked the strikes was to clear the way for a coup. Under today's fascist regime, which is massively eliminating small, medium and even big (non-monopoly) manufacturers, it is evident that their genuine interests were respected only by the popular government. The new urban middle strata, still in the formative stage, are becoming more active politically in comparison with other urban middle strata. The students, members of the liberal professions, intellectuals, and some of the army officers who may be listed as members of these middle strata are likewise gaining in social leverage.

A strong alliance has developed between the workers and students, whose mutual relations went deeper when the popular government was in power. The student movement as a whole helped the government in various ways. However, this was only one aspect of a complex process in which student groups backing the opposition became ever more aggressive. Many intellectuals too held essentially progressive views. At that time their creative thought found expression in the most diverse forms. The situation was different in the professional people's organisations. Some of them became tools of the most reactionary elements. Among the army officers there was a democratic current which lost ground as the overall situation worsened and which made no effort to strengthen its relations with the forces backing the government.

The struggle between revolutionaries and counter-revolutionaries for a favourable balance of forces was aimed to a notable extent at winning over the middle strata. But the working class failed to campaign resolutely for the demands of these strata by using the positions it held in the government.

Higher stages

Experience tells us how very important it was to bear in mind the nature of the changes taking place in Chile and typical of a democratic revolution, so that there might be no attempts at skipping stages, to carefully analyse the contribution which the strata hit by the existing contradictions could have made and to study the possibilities of the revolutionary process moving on to higher stages with the support of the majority of these strata.

A correct policy of alliance implied mutual understanding between Popular Unity and the Christian Democratic Party (CDP), a multi-class party holding strong positions among the middle strata and wielding appreciable influence among wage workers. The CDP voted for the confirmation by both chambers of Congress of Allende's election to the presidency, as well as for the nationalisation of the major copper mines, a measure unanimously approved by parliament.

From the popular government's point of view, to achieve mutual understanding meant compromising, and definite efforts were made to this end but they failed owing to resistance in both the CDP and Popular Unity. On the one hand, the opposition consisted of bourgeois and petty-bourgeois sectors prompted above all else by the fear that the working class might strengthen its positions. On the other hand, it included left-wing forces which regarded all compromise as a retreat – on the false assumption that the task was to hasten socialist changes even though the political and economic requisites were lacking. However, it was an opposition which could perfectly well have been foreseen and removed through patient work among the masses.

In Chile, as we know from experience, the achievement of mutual understanding made it possible to advance. Success in the effort to establish a broad democratic front depended in no small measure on the forces that were outside Popular Unity taking a broad approach to this question and on the nature of the trends developing among the masses, including the Christian Democrats. In noting the possibility and necessity of joint action with the Christian Democrats, the Communist Party leadership made the following points:

"To be sure, there is much that has divided and still divides the Marxists and Christian Democrats. But we also have common interests and one obvious lesson of the history of our country is that whenever we succeeded in unfolding joint action and achieving unity on the main issue, the result was specific benefits for the people.

"This is one side of the medal. But there is also the other side, for the CDP is a multi-class party in which opposed interests often make themselves felt. This explains why every time sectarian forces linked with monopoly and finding invaluable support in sectarian manifestations among the left-wing forces won the upper hand in the CDP leadership, the result was a split or even a confrontation that brought dividends to reactionary interests."[5]

Anti-fascist forces

The Communist Party says explicitly, as we see, that it was necessary to fight for unity with all anti-fascist forces. It also stresses the special significance of the ideological struggle against those who hinder or oppose the effort for unity. The struggle for unity, in which the Communist Party plays a notable part, does not imply renouncing the ideological struggle or forgetting the central task, which is to bring positions closer together by increasing the possibilities of alliance.

There is no reason why the differences existing between the CDP and Popular Unity should become antagonistic, especially if the matter is considered from the point of view of the CDP's class composition. Those who opposed the working-class policy of alliance said that the working class was thereby relinquishing its leading role and would be unable to act independently. In other words, attention was drawn to a fictitious, non-existent contradiction. After all, it is not by decree but as a result of mutual understanding with other classes and strata that the working class can become the leader, which depends on how well it carries on its activity and how far the interests of these classes and strata become its own. This is not contrary to the independent activity of the working-class party and, moreover, makes its independence necessary. Unity inside the alliance inevitably combines with struggle, above all when the alliance comprises the most diverse forces.

To strengthen the Communist Party, build up its influence and spread Marxism-Leninism are tasks whose fulfilment guarantees extension and consolidation of the alliance. This does not connote a sectarian approach; it neither presupposes an exclusive status for us, nor rules out the growth of other united front parties. To strengthen the Communist Party is not a selfish end in itself but an objective requirement of social progress. Consequently, greater unity hinges directly on the Communists' growing influence, for they win allies not only through their policy and ideology but through the strength of their organisation. This makes it still more essential for the working-class party both to maintain its class independence inside the common front and to extend its ideological influence. The period we are analysing has confirmed that this can be attained by invariably leaning on the masses, telling the working people the truth and helping them cope with difficulties and arrive at correct solutions. This is what our experience teaches us.

The nomination of a common candidate of the popular forces in 1970, the formulation of a unity programme and the definition of the basic standards of activity of the popular government were done with the people's active participation, which played the decisive role in overcoming difficulties.

However, the government did not always adhere to this principle. Many of the decisive debates on whether or not the revolutionary process was being led correctly were only held at the summit or in very narrow circles. As a result, difficulties arising from the lack of a single leadership increased, which repeatedly found expression in divisive and anarchist moves and at times tended to paralyse the government. But every time the government turned to the working people they showed a great ability to mobilise.

Stressing the importance of mass action does not mean minimising the importance of work among leaders. It would only harm our cause if we were to distinguish artificially between work among the masses and work among leaders. The foregoing invites the conclusion that one of the main problems of the Chilean revolutionary process was that no solid and homogeneous revolutionary leadership was brought into being. At the same time, the gains that were made were largely due to the process of forming such a leadership. The main role in its formation and development was played, due to the very nature of the revolutionary process, by the working class, and to the extent that the working class failed in this respect, it made things easier for the enemy.

It was also revealing that the role of the Communist Party grew as the revolutionary situation and the struggle for power developed.

We Communists take self-critical stock of both the achievements and the shortcomings of the revolutionary process in Chile so as to learn its lessons, which is a prerequisite of transforming yesterday's defeat into tomorrow's victory.

NOTES

1 Lenin, *"Left-wing" Communism – an Infantile Disorder*, Lenin Collected Works, Vol. 31, pp.70-71).

2 Orlando Millas, "La clase obrera en el Gobierno Popular". *Cuadernillo de Propaganda*, No4, pp.14-15.

3 *Boletin informative del Comite Central del Partido Comunista de Chile*. Boletin No:8, p.37, Santiago, Chile, 1972.

4 Ibid, p.33.

5 *Desde Chile hablan los Comunistas!* Ediciones Colo-Colo, 1976, p.145.

6

The Problem of Defending Popular Power

Pedro Rodriguez

The events that took place in Chile and all that befell the Salvador Allende government impel one to seek a deeper understanding of that key question of all revolutions, the question of power, and more particularly, how to defend and maintain power. The character of the historical and political conditions under which our experience of revolutionary government (with all its achievements and mistakes) was shaped, must be discerned and correctly interpreted because such knowledge is the key to learning how to deal with this problem. With us this was a question of the emergence at government level of the sector of revolutionary people's power as a result of the winning of a corresponding part of the government apparatus. It was a question of this sector's ability to combine its own work with the revolutionary drive of the masses, to guide them towards accomplishing revolutionary-democratic tasks, towards socialism.

In one or another degree the Chilean events reflect practically all the problems of Marxist-Leninist theory of revolution, of capturing and retaining power: the dialectics of using the material power of government and democracy, of people's democratic tasks and socialist goals, of the objective and subjective revolutionary factors, of national features and general laws, of the national and the international, and so on. In short, all those questions that require the unflagging attention of Communists and revolutionaries.

Our revolutionary experience shows that the laws governing the transition from an old society to a new one function irrespective of the path this transition takes. Transformation of the old state, while not an automatic process, is inevitable even though at a given stage there may be evolutionary continuity of the form of rule, ie, preservation for a time of the old form but with new content. When the working class and its allies have control of a certain sector of power, particularly if executive power has been attained, as was the case in

Chile, it is something of a paradox. In Chile the popular movement was able to concentrate its class forces *with the aid*(!) of the old government machinery. Obviously, however, for this new centralising force to become effective and capable of channelling events in a *desired direction* new methods and a new government machine were required.

Because the proletariat is in the lead it cannot stop halfway and postpone accomplishment of this task, it must extend its class influence, the influence of the popular movement to the entire government apparatus, whose natural function is to execute and defend its power, and to control it. Otherwise, the popular forces will not be free to carry out effective revolutionary transformations. In Chile, with only the government to support it, the popular movement was bound by bourgeois power extending through all the remaining organs of state. The majority of these were in bourgeois hands; legislative and judiciary power, administrative and juridical organs and their strongest levers – the armed forces and the media. Events were to show our underestimation of the fact that from the very outset the monopolies and imperialism were at a disadvantage, even in danger, because they could no longer rely on the outdated bourgeois-democratic institutions and classical political methods to restrain the growing popular movement, which had a revolutionary programme and was determined to carry it out. It was the local big bourgeoisie and imperialism which were forced to discard the old form of rule because it no longer served their class strategy.

Creation of the Popular Unity government was the popular movement's foremost achievement. Mass activity was bound up with this government, its functioning and its protection, and the urgent revolutionary transformations that it planned. The government was the deciding factor in developing the revolutionary situation and creating the socio-political conditions for clarifying the question of people's rule. The popular government was the force behind the cardinal economic reforms, effective development of democracy, broadening the popular alliance and fostering the organisation and revolutionary consciousness of the people.

The dynamic struggle of the proletariat and the popular government for revolutionary transformations, on the one hand, and, on the other, the bourgeois and imperialist resistance to the revolution and determination to restore the regime at all costs made it imperative for the sector of state power that had been won to be extended and transformed into a new type of democratic popular state. Under these conditions retention of power and defence of revolutionary gains required not just a status quo, but continuation of the revolutionary process, consolidation of people's power and presupposed specific steps in that direction.

Progress is possible only from one phase to another. In our revolution these are, first, the phase where the working class and its allies, after winning a part of state power, begin to function in the state apparatus and set up a government. Second, the phase where the popular government is in power, does not break with those institutions of the state apparatus that are still in the hands of the big bourgeoisie, and functions within the framework of the bourgeois-democratic constitution. This is the phase of initial democratic transformations when, against the background of a general upsurge of the mass struggle and the temporary shock of the reactionary forces, the socio-political situation permits the use of the constitutional methods that brought such a situation into being. The third phase, which was particularly acute and explosive in Chile, is the phase of mounting clashes and conflicts between the organs of state power in reactionary hands, and those organs of state power belonging to the people. In this phase the clash between these two opposing poles, actually two dictatorships (with dictatorship of the popular movement still in its embryonic stage) reveals a growing tendency to "break out" of the sphere of state institutions. At a certain point the popular movement, for the sake of self-preservation and to complete its transformations, itself started becoming a kind of centre of the state activities of the revolutionary masses, ie, "a power directly based on revolutionary seizure, on the direct initiative of the people from below, and not on law enacted by a centralised state power".[1]

Revolutionary situation

Now it is apparent that this should be followed by a phase where people's power aims at building a new democratic state by combining its own state activity with the activities of the broad masses of working people, the major-ity of the population. The last two phases could be separated by months, or by hours in which case the goals of both phases would have to be attained almost simultaneously. The experience of Popular Unity shows that it failed to cope with this set of problems. "Speaking concretely," said our comrades through the *Information Bulletin* of the Chile Solidarity Committee in Havana (August 1976, No. 97), "in this case, the enemy did his work while we did not do ours."

Our analysis showed that all these phases, each of which is characterised by its political content, specific balance of forces and an equally specific devel-opment level of a ripening revolutionary situation, could have happened in Chile already in the first half of 1971. This was the time of an unprecedented increase in the mass struggle, a time when objective conditions made it dif-ficult for imperialism and the big national bourgeoisie to unite and openly oppose the revolution, when the greater part of the middle strata leaned towards the popular government and the balance of forces in Latin America was very favourable to developing democracy and social progress in Chile.

There were many more similarly appropriate situations the strike in Octo-ber 1972, the "Tancazo" (uprising in the tank units) in June 1973, and so on. However, each situation was progressively more explosive and in a sense this was endangering the revolutionary cause. From all this we have concluded that a vanguard party must be able to foresee those crucial minutes when the success of the revolution, as our Vietnamese comrades say, resembles a ton hanging by a hair. The Party should see these minutes before the popular movement takes possession of a part of state power; it must be able to use the opportunity when the enemy is weakest and needs time to gather its forces that have been temporarily paralysed as a result of the people's victories, and when internal dissension prevents it from uniting in a counter-revolutionary front and planning its actions. In other words, the Party must be able to determine the "...*turning point* in the history of the growing revolution when the activity of the advanced ranks of the people is at its height, and when the *vacillations* in the ranks of the enemy and *in the ranks of the weak, half-hearted and irresolute friends of the revolution* are strongest".[2]

Only such continuity will make it possible to retain captured positions, ensure power for the alliance of progressive forces and to enter the phase clearly defined by Lenin as the period of transition to socialism.

We have learned by experience that the strategy of power must be built on consideration of the tasks of the revolutionary movement as a whole, the need to deal with them simultaneously and to direct the masses' main blow against the old society's basis and superstructure. This is the only approach to the exercise of power that can ensure success in settling the problems of the economy and democracy.

Dynamics of revolution

The Programme of the Communist Party of Chile gives a scientific definition of the concept of the revolution: "We view the Chilean revolution as a movement of the working class and organised population which, by means of the mass struggle, removes the present ruling classes from power, liquidates the old state apparatus and production relations obstructing development of the productive forces, and carries out profound transformations in the country's economic, social and political structure, opening the way to socialism."[3]

From the viewpoint of revolutionary dynamics, the necessity of smooth transition from one phase to another and the complete triumph of Popular Unity policy, it was important for the popular struggle to steadily progress and, at the proper time, become nationwide. It was just as important that the people's power, as embodied in the Popular Unity government, should combine its work with the political movement of the vast social majority, which was fully aware of the need for revolutionary transformations, and that it should be supported by this majority. This is made possible only by a national revolutionary crisis emerging on the basis of a maturing revolutionary situation.

In examining the problem of holding power and preparing conditions for taking over complete power we were convinced of the depth and timeliness of Lenin's concept of the revolution that it is the Communist Party which must show itself to be the main creative force, a force capable of guiding the masses in the developing revolutionary situation. Of course, the revolutionary situation is, in a sense, the sum total primarily of the objective changes in society. But not every revolutionary situation leads to revolution, wrote Lenin. It only becomes such a situation when subjective activity is added to objective factors. The revolutionary forces must use the revolutionary situation. "What we are discussing," Lenin wrote, "is the indisputable and fundamental duty of all socialists – that of revealing to the masses the existence of a revolutionary situation, explaining its scope and depth, arousing the proletariat's revolutionary consciousness and revolutionary determination, helping it to go over to revolutionary action, and forming, for that purpose, organisations suited to the revolutionary situation."[4]

At its 10th Congress in 1956 the Communist Party of Chile pointed out that there was a real possibility of gaining power and it is to the credit of General Secretary Luis Corvalan that he guided the Party and the revolutionary movement in that direction. Although the Party was relatively small in numbers in the early 1960s, this enabled it to win the support of the majority of working people and all the Left forces for the programme, strategy and tactics that laid the foundations for the popular victory in 1970. This is an incontestable achievement and contribution by our Party to the Chilean revolution.

The intrinsic logic and purpose of the propositions of the Popular Unity programme embodying our political line and its conscious application in those conditions helped the popular government acquire its own distinctive features and bring into sharp focus its first and most important revolutionary measures. However, because we failed to see the significance of the ensuing processes, their relation to the revolutionary situation and its becoming a national crisis, and because certain forms of struggle were absolutised and we were poorly prepared for possible alternatives, our line was narrowed down, the popular forces' chances of retaining and consolidating their sector of government reduced, and conditions were not created for the people to gain full power.

From the viewpoint of social content all revolutions involve the use of force. The theory on the state evolved by Marx and Engels and elaborated by Lenin is confirmation of this. Lenin called Engels' theory of the state "a veritable panegyric on violent revolution" and stressed that Marxism's goal was to educate the broad masses in the spirit of such a revolution.[5]

An obsolete class will never relinquish its power voluntarily without sooner or later putting up the fiercest resistance all along the line. But neither can the revolutionary proletariat be stopped once it has started the revolution. Such is the effect of this inexorable law of history, and it has been confirmed by the events in Chile.

Essentially, social coercion is nothing but a struggle between opposing, antagonistic forces, and is expressed in various forms of class struggle. So any of them, even the most peaceful, is always *essentially* coercive. These truths are also confirmed by the events in Chile.

On the basis of such a broad approach, the efforts by Communists and all revolutionaries to create conditions for a favourable balance in the armed forces acquire prime importance. This is a question of strategy. Whether or not this balance will emerge at a definite time in the form of an armed conflict between classes depends on conditions and tactics. Consequently, retaining the part of state power that has been won, developing it and advancing towards socialism without a civil war presupposes a good deal of flexibility. This is not only because of the natural instability in the situation. A balance that will prevent reaction from launching an armed struggle against the popular government must be achieved in all sectors.

Chile's experience confirms the possibility of gaining partial state power and establishing and retaining a government before a balance in the armed forces favourable to the revolution is achieved. However, *in the final analysis* the experience of the Popular Unity government has shown that it is possible to retain and broaden this partially gained power only if the mass struggle and the general revolutionary crisis will create the requisite balance, and this depends not only on the objective disunity of bourgeois forces. To a very great extent, it depends on the effective work of revolutionaries.

An interesting phenomenon was observed in Chile – at a certain stage in the struggle during the period of Popular Unity government, the opposing classes, well aware that their historical interests were at stake (no matter whether they were of an objective nature or were ideological illusions), rose above their immediate economic interests.[6]

Retaining power required energetic explanatory and ideological work to make the population fully conscious of the historical significance of the revolution and its economic achievements. As we realised, effort should have been kept up until the people themselves became convinced that the revolutionary economic achievements were well established and that Popular Unity had taken over the levers of government from reaction. At the same time attention should have been concentrated on economic changes in the people's interests. These are an important factor in stimulating consistent effort. They testify to the government's readiness to carry out its promises. They likewise consolidate and further the popular alliance and help isolate the opponents of social progress.

The economic situation in which the Popular Unity government was forced to deal with these problems was unusually complicated. The financial and landed oligarchy was still a great influence in the economy and controlled massive financial resources, a considerable part of which was intended for speculation. Many economic levers were still in its hands and it retained influence in the government bureaucracy.

The parliamentary opposition majority made it difficult, at times impossible, to pass laws that could rectify the situation. For this reason crimes of an economic nature were not legally punishable. It was also imperative to restructure the whole relationship of foreign economic dependence. This meant not only returning to Chile control of its basic resources, which were in the hands of the US monopolies, but also liquidating these monopolies' domination of the economy, particularly its most dynamic branches, changing the historically shaped geographic structure of foreign trade, establishing new international financial relations, and effecting other measures. And it was in these difficult conditions that the profound transformations envisaged in the government programme had to be carried out, the public economic sector developed, production increased, labour productivity rose, the basic principles of planning and centralised management formulated, and the masses, particularly the working people, involved in genuine economic management.

In Chile imperialism did its utmost to destabilise the popular government. Economically it resorted to a financial and technological blockade. With the help of Chile's financial clans it mounted desperate opposition inside the country, boycotting production, leaking currency abroad and speculating in capital. To this the imperialists and reactionaries added psychological warfare to intimidate the population, particularly the middle strata, create a black market, cause a shortage of consumer goods and food, and general economic chaos and anarchy. The imperialists and reactionaries were bent on preventing any balance of forces being established that would in any way be favourable to the popular government, and on isolating the latter. Imperialist strategists were fully aware of the economic and political importance of that part of the population connected with retail trade and transport and were counting on their being able to paralyse the economy and, as a result of economic manipulations by the monopolies, turn a large part of the population against the government.

Economic disruption

The Chilean events have taught the Communists the need to foresee inevitable economic problems and find ways of settling them, the need for sustained ideological work on these problems and explaining to the masses that at such times they must put duty before rights and be prepared to make certain material sacrifices for the revolution, so that together with the revolution they can finally overcome backwardness and exploitation. Ideological work must be correctly proportioned with practical activities for the revolutionary goals.

The activities of the masses and government action must be organised so as to prevent disruption of the economy. Communists must demonstrate their ability to deal with economic problems with the help of their allies, the popular masses, the socialist countries and international solidarity, and of course, above all, by their own handling of the economy.

Yet another lesson we have learned is that the ability of the Communists and their allies to defend and consolidate people's power, to find a correct solution for economic problems depends in large measure on how realistic and viable the economic programme itself is, how clearly the Communists visualise the stages of the revolution, the scope and depth of the socio-economic problems at every stage and the general rate at which transformations should be made. Revolutions cannot be tied down to any particular date. The rate at which changes take place cannot be determined by revolutionaries at will. It is determined by the actual conditions, internal and external, and these the revolutionaries must foresee.

The Salvador Allende government was the most democratic in Chile's history. It was supported by the overwhelming majority of the population, was closely bound up with their difficult struggle and was a reflection of the Chilean people's fervent desire for change. This government developed the people's democratic gains, improving their content; it gave the people a larger role in running the country and was deeply patriotic.

The popular government granted full freedom of self-expression to all sections of society. This fact is particularly important in connection with the current in-depth discussions of democracy, its class character and content. The ideological and practical activities of the popular government were centred mainly on the problem of democracy and developing the positive values and institutions that the working people had won. At the same time, it became apparent that imperialism's attitude towards freedom and democracy, and its initial "acceptance" of the people's decisions and intentions, were pure hypocrisy. For example, when the popular government was formed after the general election, the classes that were hostile to the revolutionary process, showing that they were following the "rules of the game", did not openly sabotage its work. It is an undeniable fact, however, that imperialism was preparing its conspiracy before the Popular Unity government came to power.

During the initial stage of the revolution the nature of democracy and freedom, their class essence were hidden in the shell of the prevailing legal forms, which obscured the level and content of the class struggle. At the beginning these forms restricted its development to such an extent that the popular movement was compelled to partially accept the bourgeois rules of playing democracy under which it was developing. It had to do this to demonstrate the legality of its government in the eyes of a part of society and the army. This government, however, did immediately take advantage of the existing institutions to carry out several basic transformations in the people's interests.

At the beginning this situation forced the big bourgeoisie and imperialism to express formal recognition of the popular government but did not stop them from using the institutions of state power to set up obstacles and interfere with its work.

Nevertheless, this relatively favourable balance during the first stages helped the popular government because it made way for its initiative when the time came for the more important transformations. But this balance shifted when the bourgeoisie started opposing the revolutionary changes and there began an open confrontation of hostile forces. This confrontation, at first legally regulated by the ruling classes, turned into a clash that was not regulated by any of the existing laws.

It has been shown that this struggle continues until either the new democratic development determined by the popular forces establishes a new social order or, as was the case in Chile, fascism seizes power, abolishes all democracy and launches outright terror on behalf of the big national and imperialist financial capital against all other classes, and all "play" by the class forces comes to an end. Fascism, said Georgi Dimitrov, means settling accounts with the working class by terror when its state and economic regime can no longer compete with the working class even by playing with marked cards at the bourgeois game of democracy.

The experience of our revolution has made it quite plain to us that from the point of view of retaining power and defending the revolution, the problems connected with the new scope and new essence of democracy and also the weight and strength of the new power and its state organs are of decisive importance. "As for the development of society," said Luis Corvalan, addressing a meeting in Moscow in January 1977, "our position is clear. In a society that consists of antagonistic classes all forms of rule represent an aspect of dictatorship of the ruling class, and dictatorship of the proletariat is more democratic than any form of bourgeois rule. International experience attests to this. In the light of what took place in Chile, it is imperative today to bring a popular government to power that is capable of countering all the conspiracies and coups planned by imperialism, internal reaction and fascism. The question of a dictatorship of the proletariat is not on the agenda in Chile today, but at the appropriate time it will inevitably arise, making the democratic gains more effective."

Progress towards socialism without an armed class struggle presupposes wide and vigorous polarisation of social forces. Naturally, those forces opposed to the revolution place themselves objectively outside the values of real democracy; other forces are not part of the revolutionary camp although they remain within the framework of this democracy. The popular movement carries on a political and ideological struggle to win over new forces, to defend revolutionary goals, and to launch political and philosophical discussions within the concepts of the new society. Relations with these forces and their parties, like the political and ideological struggle, may be expressed in various ways that include cooperation based on unity and a comparison of differences.

But one thing, the main thing, is clear: *democracy must serve the people and not allow freedom of action for the counter-revolutionary forces.* This is, life has taught us, one of the absolute conditions for defending revolutionary gains.

The experience of the popular government is further confirmation of the fact that the struggle can take a correct revolutionary course and assume a mass scale only if the working class maintains its leading role and class independence. We have learned that the need for a broad front cannot be replaced by a "pluralistic" approach that forfeits or weakens the leading role of the working class.

The working class and its party must wage an ideological struggle against anarchism, adventurism and right-wing opportunism, which seeks a way out of the situation through agreement with reaction. All this places a big responsibility on the Communist Party and its allies and shows the need to make a theoretical summing up of the experience of other revolutions, but above all the lessons of our own people's struggle. The Party must identify their creative potentials and learn from the experience of our allies in struggle.

NOTES

1 Lenin, *The Dual Power,* Collected Works, Vol. 24, p.38).

2 Lenin, *Marxism and Insurrection,* Collected Works, Vol. 26, pp.22-23.

3 *Programa del Partido Comunista de Chile.* Santiago, Imp. Horizonte, 1969, p14.

4 Lenin, *The Collapse of the Second International,* Collected Works, Vol. 21, pp.216-217

5 Lenin, *The State and Revolution,* Collected Works, Vol. 25, p. 399.

6 The latter were characteristic of certain intermediate social strata that were won over by reaction although they enjoyed economic advantages from the Popular Unity government.

7

Psychological Warfare:
A Political Weapon of Imperialism

Rodrigo Rojas

The very fact that Chile is living under a fascist regime shows that imperialism stops at nothing to stave off a threat to its interests. The Chilean experience, as well as impelling us to make a careful and constructive study of problems of the revolution, leads us to the conclusion that we must make a careful study of the political arsenal of imperialism and reaction.

This article attempts an analysis of only one aspect of the subject – psychological warfare as a political weapon of imperialism and examines from this point of view what happened in Chile.

Democratic rights and freedoms are admittedly a major factor for the development of the class struggle. The working class champions democratic development. The very existence of democratic rights for the people in capitalist countries today is conditional on how successfully the workers fight against imperialism, on the concessions which the ruling classes are forced to make to the working class and its allies. When the issue of reorganising society on revolutionary lines comes to the fore, reaction uses every means at its disposal against the democratic rights won by the workers.

In Chile there developed a situation in which the democratic rights of the overwhelming majority of the people could no longer be preserved, let alone extended, without stopping abuses of these rights on the part of a reactionary minority.

The forces intent on installing fascist rule launched a psychological terror campaign through the mass media to pave the way for military terror. With the campaign gaining momentum and the fascist conspiracy unfolding, propaganda and physical terror merged into one. That these two forms of terror were not stopped in time was a sign of our weakness, as events revealed.

In an open letter to President Salvador Allende of Chile on August 29, 1972, Luis Corvalan, General Secretary of the Communist Party of Chile, stated the

Communist position as follows: "Recognition of the rights of the opposition should not lead us to accept every kind of excess or misdeed.

"Some opposition spokesmen think the law can be twisted at will. There are opposition newspapers and broadcasting stations which have made lies, insult, slander, false and alarmist reports their daily bread. Our first and foremost duty to the people and the country is to put a straightjacket on those who want to drag Chile into a bloodbath. The need to maintain and assure the development of freedom and democracy binds us to use the law against those who resort to crimes with an eye to bringing down the government and setting up a fascist dictatorship."[1]

Developments proved this position correct. Furthermore, there is new evidence indicating that the propaganda machinery of Chilean reaction did not merely pursue propaganda aims but waged a psychological war preparatory to an armed struggle against the people.

The Chilean experience also shows that in exporting methods and techniques of this kind of warfare, imperialism tries in each particular case to represent them as a purely national or local matter. Yet it is obvious that the reactionary controlled media performed their part according to a "script" written by experts of the CIA and other subversive agencies of US imperialism. We find the fundamentals of this "script" in *Psychological Operations*, a manual brought out by the US war department.

Personal interests

Claiming that "peace today is a continuation of the war by non-military means", the manual describes "psychological propaganda, or psychological operations", as the principal means of this nature now in use.[2] These were planned and put into effect to influence the sentiments, attitudes or behaviour of people in other countries in a manner "favourable to the success of US policies and objectives". The purpose of psychological war, the manual notes, is to generate despondency, defeatism and apathy, encourage people to put their personal interest above the public interest and heighten their interest in private life so as to reduce their support of collective or national aims, foment scepticism regarding the political aims and ideology of the local or central authority (if these are hostile to US intentions), discord, dissent and strife, increase disarray and confusion in people's behaviour, and incite them to violent anti-social actions so as to undermine the political structure of the country and encourage resistance movements against authority.

Precepts and recommendations of this nature were used most zealously in Chile. The psychological war served to aggravate the country's serious economic problems, set the middle strata of society against the working-class movement, bring about an alliance between these strata and the big bourgeoisie on the basis of imperialist policy and establish the hegemony of financial capital in the political leadership of the counter-revolution. Reaction strove through psychological pressure to drive a wedge between the government and certain sectors of the popular movement and to foment discord in it by publicising the ultra-leftists' provocative and objectively counter-revolutionary concepts and actions. By taking advantage of the class character of the army and the fact that imperialist influence in its ranks had grown, reaction also strove to achieve in and outside the army a balance of forces that would help to move it away from the popular government, disregard the military's celebrated professionalism, "indifference" to politics and respect for civilian authority and involve them in the dirty business of a coup and crimes against the people.

This policy was combined, not without antagonisms between diverse groups of the ruling classes, with the activity of all the power centres still in their hands, which led to a veritable institutional siege of the Popular Unity government and tended to become an obstacle to the exercise of power.

The Chilean experience has shown that psychological pressure is brought to bear by such traditional means as the cinema, television, the radio or the press plus such unseemly ones as gossip, rumour and intrigues. The idea is that at a time of social upheaval rumour and gossip begin to live a life of their own as it were, acquire a dynamic quality and, spreading through society like a malignant tumour, stimulate an irrational behaviour among the masses and create an explosive situation.

Reaction uses terror as the main "supplement" to psychological pressure. Although the policy of intimidation is neither omnipotent nor reliable imperialism and its allies contrived to exploit it, causing fear and arousing hatred among certain sections of the population and directing these sentiments against the popular movement and the government formed by it. In an atmosphere of violence, which is only natural during a revolution, many are understandably gripped by fear. This sentiment also motivates the old ruling classes removed from power. Imperialism cunningly uses this situation by exploiting primarily anti-Communist prejudices instilled from generation to generation. In other words, it begins to implement a policy of intimidation primarily towards its own allies, seeing it as a means of intensifying class sentiments, causing unrest among the bourgeoisie and helping it to consolidate. This means that the purpose of the policy of intimidation at its early stage is to evolve definite forms of defending class interests so as to go over to outright anti-Communist aggression later on, when fear turns into hatred.

The policy of intimidation is also used against the working class and its most trustworthy allies. Imperialism, well knowing that this policy cannot make the politically mature section of the people change its ideological position (as numerous experiments have revealed), concentrates on measures to dampen the working people's militancy and undermine their confidence in leaders. Psychological pressure was meant to breed discord and disunity among the workers, divide them and reduce them to passivity. The mistakes and weaknesses of the popular movement itself were skilfully used as an objective factor. The ultra-leftists' action against the small and middle proprietors and the popular government, their vain appeals to the armed forces and their "leftist" talk were used in the psychological war (irrespective of the intentions of the "leftist" groups' leaders).

However, the main target of the policy of intimidation from the class point of view was the middle strata, in particular groups of the petty proprietor-minded bourgeoisie. Imperialism used psychological terror as a means of erecting an uneasy social situation and exploiting people's innate, most atavistic sentiments.

Psychological pressure was also exerted on such social institutions as the family, whose image had not yet been "tarnished" by traditional bourgeois policy. To be sure, this applied to vacillating population groups, to those who had refused to support the Popular Unity programme and were likely to side with the opposition. They were made to understand that each family should become a centre of anti-popular agitation and organisation and that they all should unite on the platform of an aggressive anti-Communist class policy. Women with a bourgeois background were expected not to dissuade men from engaging in politics, as they usually did, but to join in such activity and become zealous advocates of bourgeois policies.

Family manipulation

The result was a volte face in the attitude of certain sections of the bourgeoisie and the middle strata to the family, to women and children. An organisation called Women's Power was formed as a proponent of allegedly feminist policy. The experience of Cuban women belonging to the bourgeoisie, who had demonstrated in mourning dress in protest against the revolutionary government under Fidel Castro, as well as the experience of the "pots and pans marches" of bourgeois women against Joao Goulart in Brazil was exported to Chile and became a major manifestation of "civil disobedience" to the Allende government. Reactionary propaganda and rumour made out women to be more courageous and determined than men, thereby goading men into militant anti-Communist activity.

The shortest path to any parent's heart was linked to their desire to give their children an education and take care of their health and safety. Reaction gambled on this in the most shameless manner. Popular Unity spokesmen and Marxists were portrayed as people turning children against parents. An El Mercurio[3] ad displayed a photograph of a student and beside it, that of an armed man in a colourful "guerrilla" uniform. The caption read: "Your son or your enemy?" and to drive the idea home, the ad said: "In socialist countries, children are made to spy on their parents." Another ad reproduced an execution. "This is communism," the caption told the reader. Printed below it in capital letters were the words "Do you want that for Chile? Save Chile from communism!" Radio broadcasts harped on the same tune you heard the rattle of a machine gun, the voice of a woman shrieking: "The Communists have killed my son!" and the announcer's voice saying: "This could happen in Chile, if Chile were Communist".

Parents were urged to protect their children: "Don't let them play outdoors", "Take them to school and back".

At the same time, reaction frankly combined psychological terror with effective class organisation. The call "Chileans, unite in anger" became the main catchword of the time, repeated with inane persistence. A sizeable section of the middle strata and the big bourgeoisie was instigated to form organisations that would foment economic chaos, terror and social anarchy.

To this end, use was made of methods that had "proved their worth". The population was egged on through endless telephone calls, written notices and rumours passed on from family to family to buy large quantities of food and use the black market because goods would soon "disappear" or "cost more". People were provoked into forming queues. Necessities and other consumer goods were hoarded. Things went so far as dumping large quantities of baby foods, milk, medicines, and so on, into dustbins or rivers. All this aroused popular discontent, of course. But the blame was put on the government and the revolution. *Psychological Operations* says: "Put the blame on those in power, Propaganda is more likely to succeed in an atmosphere of social unrest."

Questionnaires said to come from Popular Unity were distributed among the middle strata of town and countryside. They included questions on how many bedrooms and beds you had and what household utensils, and whether you were willing to share your homes and property with fellow Chileans.

And when people gave in to fear they were instigated to form "self-defence" units at the level of street, neighbourhood or district. This work was often carried out by retired servicemen, which guaranteed the paramilitary organisations concerned a high standard and, on the other hand, gave the "self-defence" measures a military and "patriotic" semblance.

Headlines like "Santiago Encircled" or "MIRists Besiege Wealthy Districts" were carried along with maps of civilian communities or military areas allegedly "freed" or "saved" from MIR "seizures".[4] Children were made to set up liaison systems, telephone codes were invented and whistles made that gave a definite signal. Full-scale operational manoeuvres were held to build up fear and hostility and stimulate conspiratorial activities among other social sectors, such as the trade unions, the liberal professions, student federations and fascist-like military men. Specialists were used to set up communications and build trenches and field hospitals. The overall purpose was to create a climate of mass hysteria. The campaign was backed up with acts intended to raise panic, such as interruptions in water supply, protracted power cuts in wealthy neighbourhoods and at military posts, or broadcasts calling on audiences "to stay calm and not to give in to extremist provocation".

"Self-defence" measures were accompanied by more and more acts of open aggression: terroristic attempts on people's lives (there were 105 serious attacks between June 1972 and February 1973, with 17 Popular Unity activists killed); strikes by transport employees, shopkeepers and members of the professions; strikes by the management of copper mines appointed by imperialists and still in charge, and bourgeois movements of "solidarity" with the strikers; the seizure of an occasional educational institution under reactionary influence; "pots and pans concerts", demonstrations, rallies and reactionary marches; broadcasts by bourgeois-controlled stations assailing the government: the building of barricades and the organisation of riots in wealthy neighbourhoods, down-town districts of the capital and other cities, and so on.

It must be noted, however, that for all the efforts of imperialism, class-conscious workers kept out of anti-government actions.

The slanderous propaganda campaign of reaction combined fear, hatred and illusions about a "democratic way out" allegedly making it possible to "rebuild Chile", and urged the overthrow of President Allende. Specifically, ads said: "Women of Chile, we cannot wait till 1976 because in the next four years communism will fully establish a dictatorship of hunger. We must replace the Marxist government without delay".

Reactionary propaganda, misrepresenting those in power, spread rumours about discord within Popular Unity and the government and described the Allende government as an "oppressor" of the people. With this aim in view, it exploited every ultra-leftist outbreak, in particular the Movement of the Revolutionary Left (MIR). *El Mercurio* did not carry a single interview with a government spokesman but repeatedly made whole pages available to MIR leaders, who did not attack reaction but government measures and vented their fury above all against the Communist Party.

Negative 'leftism'

To oppose the people to the government, reaction played up the ultra-leftists' untenable economic demands and their calls for a "revolutionary pole" opposed to the government. When arguing that the country was headed for "anarchy" owing to government activity, reaction alleged that President Allende took his cue from the ultra-leftists. But when accusing the government of "totalitarianism", it imputed to Popular Unity all the negative characteristics of the MIR.

The US war department's recommendations give a clear idea of how imperialism plans disruption of the unity of popular forces. "When you cannot attack directly," its manual says, "use insinuations. Increase frictions and try to provoke disunity, stimulate dissent and internal conflicts, foment distrust and suspicion."

Besides, reactionary propaganda always tried to discredit those in power and interpreted their personal qualities in its own way. It never hesitated to fling gross insults at President Allende, resort to outright blackmail, use fake photographs, and so on. This method of psychological warfare, too, was exported by US imperialism.

The psychological war and its results had a direct impact on the armed forces and the civilian "cordon sanitaire" surrounding them. Interruptions in food supply, economic chaos, the terror campaign instigated in bourgeois neighbourhoods and at troop and carabinero stations, the formation of "self-defence" units, the atmosphere of uncertainty and the psychological manipulation of families increased the ferment among the military and its civilian surrounding. Such factors as the institutional war in parliament and in judicial and supervisory agencies, massive attacks by reactionary propaganda, "evidence" of the "unlawfulness" of the government, which was alternately charged with "anarchy" and "totalitarianism", had a strong impact on the armed forces. There were also the actions of reactionary politicians and the wives of fascist-minded army officers, who made "psychological attacks" on patriotic officers by accusing them of lack of courage, and so forth. In exerting psychological pressure on the armed forces, recourse was also had to the provocative activity of the ultra-leftists, in particular of the MIR, with its unrestrained bragging.

Imperialism saw the main purpose of these activities, as has been said, in alienating the armed forces from the popular government and isolating patriotic commanders devoted to the Constitution from their units and the officer corps while at the same time inciting the military to carry out a coup.

The struggle against imperialism and the world revolutionary process as a whole is making steady progress. The development of the socialist countries, their growing power and the increasing influence of their foreign policy attract the attention of ever larger sections of the population of capitalist and developing countries. The impact of socialist ideas and the effect of the revolutionising example of existing socialism are growing especially in the context of the deep crisis besetting the whole capitalist system. In a desperate and fruitless attempt to find a way out of this crisis, imperialism and the forces upholding the interests of multinational monopolies use their last trump card – fascism. We do not intend to look into the intricacies of fascist ideology but in view of the problems we are analysing, we would like to call attention to certain circumstances brought out by the Chilean experience.

Policy of terror

A sine qua non of reaction's every psychological manipulation was to distort reality in the people's eyes. This resulted in certain population groups coming to believe imperialist falsehoods. To quote *Psychological Operations*, it was necessary "to create and maintain credibility" without regarding "credibility" as a "synonym of the truth". The full truth was neither necessary, nor advisable; certain facts must be modified "according to the public object". However, psychological war and terror were by no means reduced to subliminal manipulation of "public objects" whose consciousness had already been prepared by decades of anti-Communist inoculation. Chile's social system and the very evolution of the process in the 1970-73 period led to a situation in which the policy of terror, like the entire previous policy of anti-Communism, gradually turned among large sections of the bourgeoisie, including part of the petty bourgeoisie, into a sufficiently coherent and systematised form of ideology.

The caste that had ruled earlier could not for class reasons have a progressive ideology. On the other hand, it was no longer in a position to use outdated, crisis-ridden democracy of the liberal bourgeois type as a means of mobilising the masses. As a result, this ideological vacuum was filled by a "policy of the irrational", which became a factor in organising and mobilising the masses and led to the appearance of the abominable outlines of Chilean fascism. It is its irrationality that enables fascist ideology to shape stereotypes of social consciousness as it pleases. The fascist state begins to operate as an expression of the nation's "will"; class conflicts are replaced by conflicts between nations, which, in turn, are regarded as living beings with their psychology and temperament and with a definite predestination inherited from their ancestors. Society is not organised on the basis of the decisive role of people's objective position in the system of social production but on the basis of such "vital organic structures" as trade union, corporation, family or state.

While racial concepts do not stand out in the ideology of Chilean fascism (due possibly to its dependent character), all the above points are present, nevertheless, in the theoretical and political utterances of Chile's reactionary ideologists. Chilean conditions gave rise to these concepts, and imperialism adapted them to its objectives through its experts in terror and psychological manipulation. Thus imperialism made a decisive contribution to the framing of the strategy and tactics of reactionary forces and to the theoretical seasoning of the social psychology of fascism.

Social consciousness

The events in Chile revealed, in our view, that in periods of social upheaval, a subjective factor such as the "morale" of aroused masses – a factor to which reaction attached strategic importance – becomes one of the most important. In seeking "destabilisation", imperialism did not lean on the ideological and scientific notions of the social consciousness of the masses, but directly influenced their emotions.

It may be said to have prevented the masses in this way from realising their interests, which would undoubtedly have prompted a substantial part of them to side with the popular government.

Experience has shown that the revolutionary working class must rely on ideological elements of social consciousness adequate to a scientific knowledge of social laws. Hence the social psychology of the masses acquires a rational basis. Revolutionary fervour, in turn, strengthens the ideological convictions of the radicalised masses. In this case, all that imperialism has to do is to influence irrational emotions and then the ideology based on them will inevitably become thoroughly irrational, destructive and unhistorical.

However, all this is a lesson to the popular movement, for we failed to give battle to the class enemy in the field of social psychology, nor did we use it to muster our own revolutionary forces. We are more aware now of the vast importance of taking account of the elements of the social psychology of the masses when analysing concrete situations. The founders of Marxism-Leninism always pointed out these factors as a permanent component of a scientifically grounded policy. Their every analysis gives a precise definition of the mood of the masses as a decisive factor in the balance of forces at a given moment.

"We could not have retained power either physically or politically (in the event of a rising," Lenin wrote. "We could not have retained it physically even though Petrograd was at times in our hands, because at that time our workers and soldiers would not have fought and died for Petrograd. There was not at the time that 'savageness', or fierce hatred both of the Kerenskys and of the Tseretelis and Chernovs. Our people had still not been tempered by the experience of the persecution of the Bolsheviks in which the Socialist-Revolutionaries and Mensheviks participated".[5]

What happened in our case was that we failed to make an adequate assessment of the energy of the masses, of the workers' sacred class hatred for imperialism and fascism.

The difficult school of anti-fascist struggle adds to the communist training of our Party, directly influences our people's social psychology and fosters their revolutionary awareness. However, we do not wish anyone to go through such a school. The Chilean people would prefer a different path but they are seething with hatred for fascism, with the hatred of a people ready to give their lives for freedom.

Theoreticians of terror and psychological warfare do not overlook the fact that the people have lost neither their political common sense, nor their indomitable critical spirit, and that the fear that had gripped some is slowly but inexorably turning into irresistible class hatred. Hence the fascist regime's dread of the people, hence also its brutal round-ups of revolutionaries and its policy of genocide and prison camps.

The people are not vindictive. They will be able, in particular, to distinguish their true enemies from those who were misled or failed to stay the murderer's hand out of cowardice-their own conscience will be their sternest judge. But, to quote Luis Corvalan: "The DINA murderers and executioners, Pinochet and his clique, whose hands are stained with the people's blood, must be punished as they deserve to be."[6]

Our strength lies in the organisation, intelligence and militancy of a people who will live up to their historical role and display proper resolve. They will use every form of struggle against their enemies to end the night of fascism and open up new vistas, such as those spoken of by President Allende.

NOTES

1 *El Siglo*, August 31, 1972, p6.

2 Quotations from *Psychological Operations* are re-translated from the Spanish original of this article.

3 *El Mercurio* was a right-wing daily newspaper owned by the Edwards clan, a major Chilean finance group that received substantial financial support from the US campaign, both corporate and CIA, against the Popular Unity government.

4 Movement of the Revolutionary Left, an ultra-left organisation that carried out numerous actions against the Popular Unity programme and tried to set up an "authority" parallel to the Allende government.

5 Lenin, *Marxism and Insurrection*, Lenin, Collected Works, Vol. 26, p.24. Kerensky, Tsereteli and Chernov were figures associated with the anti-Bolshevik groups within the Provisional Government and Soviets during the 1917 Revolution.

6 *Pravda*, 5 January, 1977.

8

The Role and Character
of External Factors

Manuel Cantero

The Popular Unity government's foreign policy combined the rich traditions of the struggle for independence with the requirements of our time: it was profoundly patriotic and consistently anti-imperialist.

To achieve political and economic independence for Chile, the popular government decided to promote – and in this it was largely successful – cooperation and friendship with the socialist countries. It also extended contacts with other countries on the basis of the right to self-determination and in accordance with the interests of the Chilean people.

This clearly expressed anti-imperialist foreign policy became the basis for promoting relations with the non-aligned countries and strengthening friendship and solidarity with dependent and colonial peoples, particularly those fighting for liberation. The popular government staunchly upheld the principle of non-interference, combated all attempts at discrimination, pressure or blockade by the imperialist powers, and waged an active and consistent struggle for peace.

The Popular Unity government's Basic Programme called for national and social liberation, struggle against the monopolies and latifundia, which were the main cause of the country's backwardness and the poverty of her working people. The programme clearly expressed the people's desire for an independent and strong Chile. The popular government's policy was organically tied in with the activities of all the progressive forces that were hewing a way to detente, peace, national independence and social progress, and met with popular support throughout the world.

President Allende's meeting with President Lanusse of Argentina came as a blow to the imperialist policy of "ideological frontiers". President Allende's visits to Peru, Mexico, Venezuela, Colombia, Ecuador, Cuba, Algeria and the Soviet Union were expressions of deep friendship and of a sincere desire for co-operation. The reception accorded President Allende at the United Nations' General Assembly in December 1972 and the wide response to the speech he delivered there were indicative of the scope and effectiveness of the popular government's foreign policy. By continuing the finest traditions of Chile's long historical struggle for independence and democracy, the popular government raised to a qualitatively new and higher standard, one fully conforming to our national interests, Chile's political, economic and cultural relations with other countries.

Never before had our country enjoyed such close, harmonious and dignified relations with the rest of the world. The various measures taken to implement this policy strengthened Chile's national independence and created more favourable conditions for carrying out profound political, economic and social reforms.

The popular government came to power and launched its initial reforms in the new setting of the changed alignment of international forces. The existence and growing strength of the socialist countries, the attractive power and growing influence of socialist ideas on peoples at widely different development levels: the foreign policy of the Soviet Union, especially its active, sustained and effective effort for peace; the example of socialist Cuba which demonstrated that similar victories and similar transformations could be achieved throughout the continent; the growing scope and multiformity of the Latin American anti-imperialist movements; the rise of the independence movement in the still existing colonies; the great role of the European working class and the constantly growing influence of the Communist parties on its struggle; lastly, the growth of the democratic movement in the citadel of imperialism – the United States.

All these facts were part of the new world situation, and they had a positive impact on the Chilean events, facilitated the victory of the people, deepened the revolutionary process and enhanced its international significance.

The development of the revolutionary process in Chile would have been inconceivable were it not for the existence of powerful forces in the world working for peace and detente. On the other hand, the sympathy, friendship and hopes engendered by the Chilean events would have been inconceivable if imperialism still held undivided sway throughout the world.

True to the principles of proletarian internationalism, the Soviet Union and most of the other socialist countries rendered Chile decisive assistance in carrying out its economic and other transformations.

The Chilean people highly appreciate this assistance, of which they had constant tangible proof. For our people could see how Soviet vessels helped increase the output of protein-rich foods, how technological processes were improved in the copper industry, how large-scale construction had begun of low-rent housing, how new agro-industrial complexes were started to help the agrarian reform, how new personnel were being trained. Cuba demonstrated its sincere fraternal solidarity by its assistance in the economic, diplomatic, cultural and social service fields. The popular government also received valuable aid from Mexico and a number of non-aligned countries. All this reflected the common objective interests of the peoples in the constantly expanding struggle against imperialism, for peace and social progress.

Thus, the foundations were laid for a continuous improvement of living standards based on the people's labour effort, the realistic possibilities of ending economic and technological dependence on imperialism with the solidarity and support of the progressive forces. That is why imperialism passed its sentence of death on the Chilean experiment.

Every passing day makes it increasingly clear that it was the interaction of imperialism and internal reaction, along with the inadequate activity of the popular movement that cut short the revolutionary process. It was imperialism that worked out and supervised the plan for systematic counterrevolutionary actions against the Popular Unity government, carried out partly by recruited agents. And it was imperialism that drew up the strategy, the stages and forms of this struggle, leaving it to the CIA to carry out its terroristic designs.

Corporate conspiracies
All aspects of imperialist activity were governed by a single strategy and supervised by a single directorate with practically unlimited funds at its disposal. These facts were confirmed in a report of the US Senate Commission headed by Senator Frank Church which investigated CIA activity in Chile when the Popular United government was in power.

The following had an active part in formulating and concretising policies directed against the popular government: the National Security Council and its "Committee of 40" which coordinated the activities of certain government departments the intelligence agencies, the Pentagon, State Department and armed forces (the committee's chairman was Henry Kissinger and every move it made had the consent and direct approval of President Nixon).

Part of this destructive mechanism was exposed by President Salvador Allende with the publication of the secret ITT documents, among which were carefully prepared plans to prevent Allende's assumption of the presidency in 1970.

Action against the popular government was planned and prepared over a number of years. For example, in 1965 the country was shocked by the Communist Party's exposure of the real aims of the social research plan known under the code name of "Project Camelot". The idea was for Chilean universities jointly with the Pentagon and the American University in Washington DC to analyse Chile's revolutionary potential and, undoubtedly, take the necessary counter-measures. Throughout these years imperialism employed a wide range of techniques: the Peace Corps was used as an information centre and for penetration of the masses; American trade-union organisations were used to penetrate and split the Chilean trade-union movement; some of the research conducted by Chilean universities was financed from the United States, etc.

The "Committee of 40" began working in Chile long before Allende's election, and after that bourgeois propaganda made a special point of instilling the idea that imperialist activity was in retaliation to the measures taken by the popular government against American interests. The Church Report recorded that the "Committee of 303", the predecessor of the "Committee of 40", discussed practical measures to prevent the victory of the people in the presidential elections.

One of these measures, the most effective one, was penetration of the armed forces through a variety of methods and techniques. The reactionary "Hemisphere Security" strategy was used for systematic anti-Communist conditioning of the army and preparation of cadres to combat "subversion". Everything was done to use the army in the interests of the imperialists.

In 1952 the treasonous Videla government concluded a bilateral defence agreement with the United States, thus bringing our country into the American military aid programme. A while later, after the victory of the Cuban revolution, most of the aid was directed to Chile in order to prepare its armed forces to suppress "risings", that is, fight their own people. In fact, Chile was receiving more "aid" both on a total and per capita basis than any other Latin American country. In 1950-68, 2,064 Chilean servicemen underwent training in the United States and 549 more in the Panama Canal zone. According to official US documents, the Panama training programme was stepped up in 1968 and again in 1970-73. This was accompanied by a bigger supply of military hardware.

Military subversion

The Church Report records that in July 1969 "the CIA station in Santiago requested and was granted permission to launch a secret programme envisaging the organisation of an intelligence network in the Chilean armed forces for preparation of a coup d'état. The programme was in operation for four years and included the recruitment of agents in the three armed services of the Chilean Army.

They were drawn from regimental commanders to lieutenants, from retired generals to officers of the administrative service, and among privates. Towards the close of 1971 and early in 1972 the CIA intensified its army penetration programme. Reports by the intelligence services on progress in planning a coup d'état noted two probable crucial periods: one, in the last week of June 1973 (for "El Tancazo "tank strike" – MC) and another at the close of August and the first two weeks of September."[1]

Imperialism systematically financed political leaders, reactionary newspapers, also trade union and student organisations throughout the continent. The "Committee of 40", the Church Report says, assigned large sums to support the opposition media in their "hard-line" propaganda campaigns. This "aid" was given on the spurious pretext that freedom of the press was endangered by the popular government. The Inter American Press Association, made up of the continent's most reactionary media, acted along much the same lines. According to CIA documents cited in the Church Report, this played a considerable part in preparing the climate for the 1973 military coup.[2]

Overthrowing the popular government was a top priority of imperialism.

And not only because it wanted to hold onto its economic interests in Chile, but mainly because it was anxious to prevent the spread of the Chilean revolutionary experiment to other countries and, more especially, prevent its influence on the future of Latin America. This is clearly evident from a memorandum drawn up by the CIA a few days after Salvador Allende was elected president.

"As for the threat to US interests," the memorandum says, we have come to the following conclusions: 1. The United States has no vital national interests in Chile. Nonetheless, economic losses would be considerable; 2. The world balance of military forces would not be considerably disturbed by the coming to power of the Allende government; 3. Allende's victory, however, would involve considerable political and psychological losses: a) its coming to power and the reaction it would evoke in other countries, the challenge this would present to the OAS could jeopardise unity of the Hemisphere . b) Allende's victory would represent a definite psychological defeat for the United States and a decisive psychological success for the Marxist ideology."[3]

The international reverberations of Chile's revolutionary process spurred imperialist action, for it demonstrated the realistic possibility of a peaceful takeover of power by the people and the introduction of deep-going structural changes into the bourgeois government machine.

While pursuing its main aim, imperialism was of course anxious to defend the interests of the big multinationals operating in Chile. In 1970, Chile was a dependent country relying largely on a mono-commodity export trade. A very considerable share of imported goods, especially strategic goods, came from the United States. Chile's financial system was an appendage of America's. The traditional trade and balance of payments deficit was covered by more foreign loans and by the unlimited and unrestricted flow of foreign capital, especially into the basic industries.

In the 1960s imperialism intensified penetration of the more dynamically developing industries, but the US monopolies also retained their traditionally strong positions in mining. In 1968 foreign concerns controlled more than one-sixth of invested capital in manufacturing: 61 of the country's 100 leading enterprises had foreign capital, and 40 of them were entirely under foreign control.[4]

All this meant high profits for foreign investors. Speaking on the day the big copper mining companies were nationalised, President Allende emphasised that the profits received by the US companies between 1930 and through 1970 added up to US$1,576 million, and the loss caused by export revenue not returning to Chile over the same period amounted to US$2,673 million, though the initial investments of these foreign companies were between 50 and 80 million dollars.[5]

Other multinational concerns, for instance, ITT, which played such a prominent part in engineering the coup, were enjoying constantly increasing profits. More, a commission appointed to investigate ITT operations in Chile found that just before the popular government took over it was preparing to penetrate many other branches of the economy cellulose and paper, electronics and electrical equipment, copper processing, tyres, saltpetre, even low-rent housing and salt.[6] Imperialism was using every available means to undermine the reforms Chile was carrying out, but it was most of all concerned to prevent the spread of the "Allende doctrine" to other countries. And the spread of the Chilean experiment in nationalising the big copper companies would have had very unhappy results for the multinationals operating in other dependent countries.

The imperialists knew only too well that if our nationalisation reform succeeded, it would have reverberations far beyond Chile. More, at a time when imperialism was making a desperate effort to prevent nationalisation of basic resources in dependent countries, and with the peoples and governments of Afro-Asian and Latin American countries energetically resisting such attempts, the spread of the Chilean experiment could prove decisive.

Nationalisation of foreign investments in Third World countries would be a telling blow to the multinationals, all the more painfully felt by them because nationalisation involves not only their assets, but also the profits they made over and above what is considered a normal level. And so, the "Allende doctrine", based precisely on that principle, would undermine the very foundations of imperialist capital.

Monopoly profits

The constitutional reform on nationalisation of the big copper companies, unanimously approved by parliament, authorised the President to decide on full or partial appropriation of excessive profits in determining compensation payments to foreign companies (this involved the annual profits of North American monopolies in Chile beginning with May 1955). President Allende was also empowered to determine profit norms, and everything above these was regarded as excessive profit. This enabled Chile to get back at least part of the huge profits amassed by the US monopolies over 15 years.

The profits of the North American monopolies "repatriated" to the US were several times bigger than their investments in Chile. More, Anaconda and Kennecott (the main US exploiters of our copper deposits) were earning more in Chile, much more in fact, than in any other part of the world. For instance, in 1955-70 one of Anaconda's Chilean subsidiaries was making an annual profit of 21.5%, compared with only 3.6% in other countries. Kennecott did even better – its annual average profit was 52.8% and in some years as high as 100%, in fact in 1969 it topped the 200% mark, compared with only 10% in other countries.

To quote President Allende: "The profits of some of the nationalised enterprises over the past 15 years had reached truly colossal dimensions, so that after the introduction of moderate restrictions on profit – 12% per annum – we were able to hold back considerable sums".[7] And after these sums were subtracted from the compensation payments, both Anaconda and Kennecott were in debt to the Chilean government.

To prevent the Chilean experiment from spreading to other dependent countries, the US monopolies and government launched a gigantic pressure campaign against Chile. Anaconda imposed an embargo on Chilean assets in the United States. Kennecott sequestered a consignment of Chilean copper and sold it in France, the Netherlands and Sweden. The idea, of course, was to prevent Chile from earning foreign exchange by disorganising the export of copper and thus stifle the country by a financial blockade.

Time magazine (November 6, 1972) commented: "Obviously, Kennecott's offensive is likely to hurt future copper sales to customers unwilling to risk legal hassles and possibly costly delays in deliveries.

"Kennecott officials are determined to keep the heat on Chile. The Manhattan office of General Counsel Pierce McCreary, who is directing the campaign, has the air of a war room. His desk is strewn with shipping reports, and on one wall hangs a large map for plotting ships' courses.

"At present he is monitoring the movements of at least six ships headed for Europe, loaded with El Teniente metal; when they arrive he wants his agents to be there to greet them with court orders."

It was perfectly clear that the multinational monopolies whose interests were most affected were not the only parties to this concerted offensive. The US government tried to make a review of Chile's foreign debt conditional on the payment of compensation to the US monopolies, though this was clearly contrary to the constitutional nationalisation laws.

Washington also made this a condition for Chile receiving loans from such international financial organisations as the World Bank and International Monetary Fund.

This offensive against nationalisation of copper and the "Allende doctrine" did not come as any great surprise: whenever the imperialists find that their interests are in danger, they are prepared to wage a desperate last-ditch fight. To counter that, Chile had to pursue a foreign policy of a new type, one that accorded with its national interests in foreign trade and safeguarded its foreign-exchange reserves. All this, naturally, was directly linked with the reforms then being carried out and designed to assure an independent foreign policy.

Nationalisation of copper, iron and saltpetre meant that a substantial part of our export trade passed to state agencies. In 1971 they accounted for 84% of all exports and the target for 1973, which was being successfully attained, was 93%. And this was the picture in imports: state agencies accounted for 55% of all imports in 1971 and for as much as 76% in 1973. State control was of particular importance in planning and developing foreign trade and in rectifying its deformed structure (by reducing the share of the United States and promoting trade relations with other countries), and also in countering aggressive imperialist policies.

Copper nationalisation, and nationalisation of banking, also enabled us to take a long step towards centralising the management of our currency reserves most of which had been locked up in Anaconda and Kennecott accounts in foreign banks. We had thus made significant progress in centralising the management of foreign trade and foreign exchange operations. A state foreign trade structure was gradually taking shape and this, coupled with other measures, enabled the government to reshape its international relations.

And if imperialism was able, in the end, to organise such effective and large-scale counter-revolutionary actions against the popular movement, it was because the measures introduced by the revolutionary forces and their allies were not resolute enough. There was, in effect, an obvious underestimation of the main enemy, due to inadequate theoretical and practical understanding of the role and danger of imperialism.

This miscalculation should be seen in the context of our relative lack of thorough knowledge of the main structural features of Chilean society. And this, in turn, was basically due to overestimation of some of the specifics of Chilean society: on the one hand, there were exaggerated notions about revolutionary change being brought about on the basis of a dubious legality, on the other, there was the opinion that the working class could assure, single-handed, without any outside assistance, the successful advance of the revolutionary process.

In the final analysis, the existence and role of these erroneous views were due to underestimation of the importance for the revolutionary forces fully to rely on the masses.

There was also this negative factor: the biased attitude of some circles to the solution of economic problems as a key element in the fight for power, and underestimation of the importance, at such a crucial time, of assistance from the socialist countries. In practice, this created conditions for the subversive activities of imperialism and the oligarchy, particularly in the economy, and for the growing influence of "destabilisation" on all aspects of our national life.[8]

Economic dependence

The "destabilisation" policy, so consistently carried out by imperialism, was based on accurate knowledge of Chile's economic structure, its limited potential, the result of long years of vulnerable dependence. When Nixon said that the Chilean economy must be "made to scream" this was not a hollow phrase. The dependence bonds were very strong and breaking them was a difficult and complex job. Suffice it to say that in 1955-70, 37% of all our imports, and about 50% of producer goods, came from the United States. But even these figures do not give an accurate picture of what the decision "to prevent a single bolt or nut from reaching Chile" really meant for our country. To understand all the consequences of that decision one must bear in mind the composition of our imports, which included many items unobtainable at home. More than 90% of equipment for the copper industry and 87% of spare parts for the oil industry had to be imported from the United States; the position was much the same in mining.

Traditional financial dependence on the US was especially onerous. Practically all short-term financial operations were conducted through the big American banks and on their terms. Long-term credits came mainly from the US government or from the international financial institutions that were largely dominated or strongly influenced by it. Furthermore, these loans were granted only if they suited imperialism's interests and aims in Chile.

In compliance with the "destabilisation" policy, US banks suspended short-term financing: from an estimated total of more than US$300 million prior to September 4, 1970, the figure soon dropped to only US$32 million. Most of the international credit organisations, which take their cue from the US government, virtually stopped granting credits. In trade, "destabilisation" led to growing difficulties in imports, even from third countries. To this should be added the embargo and other measures taken to block exports of Chilean copper and other goods.

The economic blockade caused much damage. And there can be no doubt that the problems posed by "destabilisation" made these things easier for the putschists, enabling them, among other things, to rely on certain sections of the population. Nonetheless, the blockade was, in the main, foiled. This is important, because it shows the opportunities open, in the present international setting, to countries like Chile to pursue an independent policy in the fight against imperialist economic aggression.

Gradually, we succeeded in radically changing the geographical pattern of our foreign trade. Imports from the US were drastically cut and we obtained raw materials, spares and machinery from other countries. With the exception of the Kennecott embargo, exports continued on a normal course. We also substantially altered the system of short-term financing by concluding agreements with banks in the socialist countries and some Latin American and European capitalist countries.

The failure of the economic blockade demonstrated – and this has been confirmed by the revolutionary process in Cuba and in a number of other countries – that the US monopolies are no longer omnipotent. Now, with the changed world balance of forces, any country that has decided to follow an independent course and has broken out of imperialist dependence, can rely on support from many quarters. First, it can count on the support of the socialist countries. The example of Chile has also demonstrated that there are opportunities for wider economic intercourse with Latin American countries. True, they are not being fully used, because these countries' economic relations are mostly with the United States. Our experience has also shown that, due to the contradictions within the imperialist camp, economic relations can be established with some of its countries. Chile's relations with a number of developed capitalist countries progressed normally, and in some cases were substantially extended.

International solidarity with the Popular Unity government was manifested in many different forms, from exposure of such imperialist machinations as the embargo on Chilean copper exports to third countries, to the organisation of a "Solidarity Museum" to which world-renowned artists contributed their works.

International solidarity with our people after the fascist coup is inseparable from the international significance of popular rule in Chile. And this solidarity involved wide segments of the public, without any concessions on principle matters on our part. On the contrary, this solidarity was the result of the consistent international policy pursued by the government of Salvador Allende.

Popular Unity, that broad political and social alliance, was forged, won power, carried out deep-going transformations, steadily extended its relations with the USSR and never made any concessions to anti-Sovietism.

The existence of popular government in Chile and its successes came as an inspiration to all peoples battling for independence and social progress. Chile's experience demonstrated anew and in a very practical way that imperialist blockade and sabotage create many difficulties, but they are not insurmountable when the consciousness and efforts of the people are merged with solidarity and assistance from all parts of the world.

NOTES

1 "lnforme de la Comision Church". *Boletin Informative,* Comite Chilena de Solidaridad la Habana-Cuba, No. 84, 1976, pp. 10, 12.

Original documents from the Church Committee in English can be found here: www.aarclibrary.org/publib/contents/church/contents_church_reports.htm

2 Ibid.

3 Ibid, No. 85, 1976, p.6.

4 *Boletin Mensual Banco Central de Chile,* No. 518, April 1971.

5 *Salvador Allende, Discursos,* Editorial de Ciencias Sociales, La Habano, 1975, p.131.

6. *Principios* No146, julio-agosto 1972, p.51.

7 *Salvador Allende, Discursos.* p.536.

8 See the article by Orlando Millas, *World Marxist Review,* November 1975.

Above: Luis Corvalan, general secretary of the Chilean Communist Party, at a central committee plenary meeting, 1972. Below: Victor Jara and family. Jara was the country's most famous folk artist and a lifelong Communist. He was murdered by the fascists in the aftermath of the coup.

9

The Unarmed Road of the Revolution:
How it worked out in Chile

Luis Corvalan

Eleven years after the Cuban Revolution, which put the Cuban people in power, a revolution was carried out by the Chilean people, who won a partial political power. This position was held for three years by the Popular Unity government, which put through the basic structural transformations of an anti-imperialist, anti-oligarchic revolution with a socialist vista.

There was interest all over the world in the changes brought about in that period, and especially in the fact that the revolution took the peaceful road, which we Chilean Communists prefer to call the unarmed road (because it is, in practice, not all that peaceful).

This interest was further increased by the fact that the government headed by President Allende had been created by a popular movement involving several parties and different democratic trends rallied round a common programme.

It was Marx who first predicted the possibility of a peaceful revolution. In 1917, the Bolsheviks, led by Lenin, twice brought up the question of the revolution's peaceful development and acted accordingly. Lenin gave it much attention, although he believed that in the conditions of the period such an eventuality would be extremely rare. Because of the new conditions which have now taken shape, the international Communist movement believes that it is more probable today.

In Chile, following Popular Unity's victory in the 1970 elections, the possibility became a reality. Whereas in the course of some other revolutions taking the peaceful road, the process was short-lived or went forward in specific conditions, directly after the rout of Nazism, in our country the real possibility of such development was borne out by the experience of three years.

The Chilean revolution has suffered a temporary reverse, but such an outcome does not refute the assumption that in other countries, and perhaps even in Chile itself, the working class and its allies will be able to win political power and carry out their revolution without resort to the use of arms.

That is why revolutionaries in many countries have been making a close study of the Chilean experience. We, for our part, believe it to be our duty to draw substantial conclusions from the whole development of the revolutionary process, which we successfully promoted over a long period, and to analyse the causes of the defeat.

The Chilean people won a part of the state power, securing the post of President of the Republic, instead of a "solid majority in Parliament", as suggested, for instance, by the 1960 Statement of the Meeting of Communist and Workers' Parties, when formulating its thesis about a peaceful road for the revolution. While remaining fully convinced of the significance and relevance of that Statement, I recall what it says merely to emphasise that the reality is richer and more varied than any theses, however basically correct these may be, and to stress the multiplicity of the forms, methods and ways of the revolution, of which Lenin spoke in his lifetime when showing the great scope of the Marxist doctrine.

Defeat reaction

But essentially our experience consists in something else. It has confirmed that the working class is capable of carrying out a revolution along any path provided it promotes the development of the class struggle, concentrates fire on the chief enemies, and helps to accelerate the changes which have matured in society, thereby rallying a majority of the people, and creating a balance of forces which enables it to defeat reaction and to tie its hands.

A plenary meeting of our Party's Central Committee in August 1977 reached this conclusion: the Chilean experience testifies that the question of "who beats whom" depends above all on who succeeds in isolating whom from the masses, and who ultimately turns out to be stronger: the working class and its allies or reaction and its allies. All the problems of the Chilean revolution, both those it did and did not solve, were linked up with this question.

The working class and its allies, the Popular Unity bloc, took the first step to power – the winning of the post of President of the republic – in the 1970 elections, when they gained a majority, but only a relative majority. The fact is that Salvador Allende won with 36.3% of the poll, that is, a larger percentage than the other two candidates for the post. This did not in itself settle the matter of filling the presidential post. For one thing, in a situation in which none of the candidates managed to win an absolute majority, the final decision rested with Parliament.

Secondly, and this is the most important point, the 36.3% result showed that the working class and its allies had to win over fresh social sections and to enlarge the framework of their alliance to achieve a correlation of forces that would make it possible for their candidate to fill the presidential post and to get down to bringing about the changes outlined in the Popular Unity Programme. This became an urgent need when it transpired that imperialism and Chilean reaction were planning to prevent Salvador Allende from assuming the post of head of state.

This was clear to all the Popular Unity parties and they began to act accordingly. Masses of working and other people thronged the streets. Everywhere efforts were made to establish contact and mutual understanding with the democratic circles which, while not voting for Allende, were still inclined to accept his victory. These circles were motivated by various considerations: some held to the tradition of backing the man who had won a majority, others feared the people, who were not inclined to give up their victory, but most found affinities with the Popular Unity programme congenial and preferred Allende to the right-wing candidate, who had come second.

Consequently, in practice, the relative majority was converted into an absolute majority. The balance of forces had tilted in favour of Popular Unity, preventing the isolated right-wingers from strangling the revolution in its cradle. Their sorties in that period failed militarily mainly because the right forces had been routed politically.

A report to our August plenary meeting said: "The successes scored within the 60 crucial days, from the Presidential elections to Allende's assumption of the post of President of the republic, and also the successes scored within the whole initial period of about a year were due, on the one hand, to the broad nationwide support for the immediate goals of the popular movement, the rallying of the masses to attain these goals, and Popular Unity's solidarity and cohesion in that period on the main issue, and on the other hand, they were due to the fact that Popular Unity had sought and found agreements and compromises with other forces that proved to be objectively necessary."[1]

Such agreements were reached with the Christian Democrats. The first of these was the constitutional guarantees pact. Later an agreement was concluded on a constitutional reform relating to the nationalisation of the major copper mines.

Some left-wingers at home and abroad took a dogmatic and even anticommunist stand and denied the very possibility of the Chilean people's winning without resort to arms. Others held that our victory had been the result of a mistake by the Right in running a candidate of their own in the 1970 Presidential elections, something they had not done in 1964. The truth is that the popular victory in 1970 resulted from a long and intense political battle for the unity of the working class, for mutual understanding between the Socialists and the Communists, for unity of the popular parties and joint action by the broadest democratic circles. The victory was also due to the political and ideological struggle against the "left" and right trends within the Popular Movement, to the correct understanding and definition of the character of the Chilean revolution and its stages, the precise formulation of programme goals and the identification of the chief enemies and of the principal and secondary contradictions in Chilean society.

The change in the correlation of forces in favour of Popular Unity following Allende's election sprang largely from that protracted and intense struggle, which had helped not only to unite the broadest sections of the people round Popular Unity but also to bring it closer to other social and political forces. During the presidential campaign, the Christian Democrats, as with Popular Unity, had advocated important goals such as the nationalisation of the major copper mines and completion of the agrarian reform. Many Christian Democrats, in view of their own experience, also believed that it was necessary to deepen the transformations and their candidate, Radomiro Tomic, even declared that capitalism was incapable of solving the country's problems. That being so, it became possible, after the elections, for the Christian Democrats and Popular Unity to reach agreement and establish mutual understanding among the broadest democratic circles, thus tilting the balance of forces in the people's favour.

The Chilean working class and people worked hard, taking creative initiatives and carrying on a selfless struggle for the success of the popular government and implementation of its programme. The working people, the young, the women, and workers in the arts displayed heroism in their labour effort, in organising the new order, in the distribution of food, of which there was a shortage, and in combating reactionary attacks.

The revolution showed once again that it helps to release much creative energy and that the people are capable of great exploits for the sake of a better future. To the very end, millions of Chilean men and women worked for that purpose.

Study mistakes

It is well known that any revolution is fraught with the danger of counter-revolution, which breaks loose whenever the revolutionaries lose the initiative, whenever the revolution begins to mark time and goes over to the defensive and when the correlation of forces eventually changes in favour of its enemies. In Chile, this occurred after the period of upswing in the popular movement and large-scale democratic transformations, after a period of successes and advances, in the course of which the popular government's policy enjoyed considerable support among the masses.

The situation changed under the impact of various factors. Some of these – like the excessively high prices of imported goods and the substantial fall in the price of exports – were beyond the control of the government and Popular Unity. These factors and especially the plans of the enemy, which was still doing its worst, were objectively the overriding ones.

But the main thing for us revolutionaries is to analyse the deep-going causes of the people's defeat, to study our own mistakes, which enabled imperialism and reaction to reach their objectives.

Popular Unity brought together in its ranks – and still does – forces which differ in social substance and have different ideologies: Marxists, rationalists, Christians. This has been and continues to be a positive fact, reflecting the scope of the alliance that has been built up round the working class. The people's strength lay in the unity of such a coalition. But for that unity to be firm it has to rest on a common programme and also to have a united and correct political leadership, which is firmest of all when the working class has the prevailing role within it. Everything on the whole went well so long as such leadership was provided and so long as a resolute struggle was carried on to fulfil the programme. When these requirements were met only half-heartedly, things began to fall apart.

We participants in the popular movement were not in agreement on all the issues. As the revolution began to run into difficulties, unity of plan and action became even more imperative. But this was precisely when the discrepancies tended to become most acute. Within Popular Unity, differences on a number of problems tended to grow, and this jeopardised the policy of uniting the whole people round the working class.

As a result the real force of the process was undermined. The programme gradually lost its edge. Instead of using all the available forces of the popular movement to deal resolute blows at imperialism, the monopolies and the land-owning oligarchy, a struggle was also started against the middle strata, a part of which had been won over to our side, and another, neutralised at the initial stage.

Reaction was able to mount its offensive when – largely because of the mistakes in political leadership – it managed to escape from its isolation and to set up a front together with these middle strata, spreading its influence even to some groups of workers. Not everyone realised that the strength of the government and Popular Unity lay in the fact that it had its own programme, a strategic basis for correct political leadership. When this correct line won out, the people found the strength to isolate and rout the enemies. But when departures from the programme, in effect, turned into a second programme, the differences on the main issues largely hampered the activity of the government and Popular Unity. This was when the situation began its rapid deterioration, which culminated in the coup.

In our view, from the day of the 1970 Presidential elections right up to the final minute of popular government, the struggle for the revolution was a struggle to change the balance of forces in favour of the people. Let us note that the favourable-balance-of-forces concept does not imply winning a majority in general, but above all an active majority. The urge to win a majority is always important, but a mere majority is obviously not enough, and may even temporarily be lacking at some moment. That is why there is much more to the complicated concept of the favourable balance of forces. Alongside the other factors, it takes account of the militant spirit, level of organisation, capability of the masses to muster their strength, homogeneity of views within the coalition and a relevant military component.

The outcome of our revolution was not, of course, fatally inevitable. The differences, which evidently exist in any coalition, need not necessarily prevail. They can be overcome, and this requires, besides a correct programme and correct political leadership, sustained participation by the masses, because the revolution is their own creation.

In Chilean conditions, the main issue in the revolution – the winning of complete power – depended on the capacity of Popular Unity to isolate the enemy and create a superiority that would make it possible to go on from the winning of the Presidential post to the assumption of control over the whole state apparatus and a profound transformation of all its institutions.

Reaction seeks to depict the revolutionary goal of winning complete power by the people as sinister, totalitarian and anti-democratic. In fact, the very opposite is true. When setting ourselves such a task, we revolutionaries act for the sake of the most noble and democratic goals. Such important components of the bourgeois state as the courts, the armed forces, the prosecuting agencies and the key instruments of economic direction are beyond real democratic control, for the people have no say in their formation or activity.

Consequently, the whole point is to secure for the working class and the rest of the people access to every organ and institution of the state so that they will eventually pass into the hands of the people. This is not some devious plot, as the reactionaries claim, but the people's use of democratic forms, methods and ways, chosen and supported by the people themselves. One could say that the winning of complete power is the only true way of making the idea of democracy a material reality, something which was so aptly expressed by Lincoln in his concept of "government of the people, by the people, for the people".

In Chile, it turned out to be possible to isolate the enemy and prevail over its forces in order to achieve a number of revolutionary objectives: nationalisation of the major copper mines and the large monopolistic enterprises and banks, completion of the agrarian reform, and establishment of control over virtually the whole of foreign trade. But no such superiority was achieved in tackling the revolutionary tasks of winning complete power, and this happened mainly because the majority of the people had pinned their hopes on the issue of control of the government rather than on control of all the power.

Broad masses of people were unaware of the need to win complete power, which was due to the inadequate political education of the masses over a period of many years and for this we Communists feel a special responsibility. As a result, we did not have at our disposal the relevant active force capable of mustering its strength for the complete solution of this problem.

When we proposed, say, the establishment of popular tribunals, which was a limited measure but would have in effect served partially to democratise the judicial machinery, or when we intended to set up a unified national system of education, which would have helped to democratise it, the enemy used the absence of any clear notion among the masses about the necessary institutional transformations, so that we were forced to retreat and abandon these initiatives.

The intention which informed these initiatives was laudable but if they were to become a reality, the majority had to understand their substance. In that concrete situation, it was a mistake to put forward tasks that would have divided the government support front. Subsequent events clearly showed the masses the class character of the Parliament, the judiciary and the military institutions. But by then the correlation of forces had deteriorated, and this made it impossible to undertake fruitful efforts – although by then the majority had come to realise the need for them – to solve the problem of power (including, of course, the democratisation of the military institutions, within which there were some supporters of change, however few).

The working class and other forward-looking forces strove to create a new type of state. Some new forms of power emerged: administrative, production and vigilance committees were set up at the enterprises which the state had taken over; the trade unions had united in industrial belts; and consumers had set up supply and price-control councils. But these embryos of the new power – and such experience is highly valuable – were not properly developed. At that time, the development of the situation was altered by the reactionary escalation. The real popular power was also weakened and the enemy moves facilitated by the acts of the ultra-leftists, who sought to turn the emergent organisations into a power alternative to the Allende government.

Meanwhile, the popular government's successful activity was exceptionally important for the development of the revolutionary process. There was a need to show that the emergent system was opening the floodgates for the development of the productive forces, for economic growth, for a better distribution of the national income and for raising the people's living standards, that is, for the country's progress and for social justice. Confirmation of this came from the running of the industrial enterprises at full capacity, the growth of production on that basis, and the rising incomes of the working people, the small and middle businesspeople and the traders.

Policy of destabilisation

However, there came a point at which higher labour productivity became crucial. The working people, guided by our Party's line, had launched many valuable initiatives and expended much effort to win the battle for production at the enterprises taken over by the state and also in the countryside. The Popular Unity government's full victory in tackling the economic problems would have attracted most of the people even more broadly and firmly to its side. This would, in turn, have helped tremendously in successfully solving the problems connected with the winning of complete power. But reactionary sabotage in production, the policy of destabilisation pursued by US imperialism and also neglect of economic problems and the lack of any genuine direction of the economy ultimately tipped the scales against us. That is the light in which the question of power appeared in Chile.

The Chilean revolution shows that, whatever direction the process takes, the hegemony of the working class and the leading role of its vanguard are the crucial factors.

The hegemony of the working class is secured in struggle and is recognised by other classes and social sections only when it exists in fact. This is achieved whenever the working class pursues a consistent policy of alliances and is successful in this field.

Winning over the petty bourgeoisie, the middle strata and the semi-proletarians has become one of the main factors in the struggle to build up a balance of forces favourable to the revolution. In a country like Chile these social forces are numerous and important. They are by no means homogeneous. The main element is the peasants, along with the impoverished sections of the population, the small traders and businesspeople, craft-workers, professional people, intellectuals, students, and so on. We may also include wage workers who do not come under the heading of proletarians. At a time of revolutionary change the tendency of these strata to waver between the positions of the proletariat and reaction becomes strikingly apparent. Some of them sided with the popular movement throughout the revolutionary process in Chile but it was a constant struggle to win over the majority of these strata. From giving a certain degree of support for, or remaining neutral towards, the government, as was the case in the initial period, most of them went over to the counter-revolution in the final period. This prompted the general conclusion that such negative shifts are inevitable. It has been claimed that as soon as the intermediate strata come up against the real possibility of radical changes, most of them fall back into the arms of reaction in order to preserve their "relative privileges". So, it is argued, Popular Unity should not try to better its previous achievement and should content itself with the support of the minority of these strata.

This conclusion is incorrect. It is clear that the conditions of life of the majority of peasants and also people compelled to migrate to the towns (a particularly intensive process in Chile) and therefore obliged to live on casual earnings, and the conditions of life of other strata of the population are comparable to those of the proletariat, and sometimes worse. Only in joint action with the working class can these strata gain a fitting place in society and improve their prospects. Only the victory of the working class can finally solve their problems. Hence there is always a possibility of achieving an alliance and mutual understanding with them.

Intermediate strata

Certain contradictions exist between the petty bourgeoisie and the working class. There can be no doubt, however, that the petty bourgeoisie is also a victim of the policy of the monopolies and the concentration of capital in the hands of the financial oligarchy. The contradictions between the petty bourgeoisie and big capital tend to deepen and this makes the possibility of its mutual understanding with the proletariat all the more likely. So the question is to achieve such an understanding.

In the course of the Chilean revolution this should have been achieved by strict observance of a programme that took into consideration the interests of the intermediate strata and indicated the direction of the main blows of the popular forces – against imperialism and the oligarchy. And in the first period of the popular government, when it kept to the programme, the attitude of these strata towards the revolution was positive.

On the political plane establishing mutual understanding meant finding channels for agreement between Popular Unity and Christian Democracy, whose supporters came mainly from the middle strata. This was particularly important because such a policy tended to strengthen the unity of the working class, where the Christian Democrats had and still have considerable influence. In our view the proletarian line of making broad alliances, far from increasing bourgeois influence on the working class, actually liberates it from such influence.

The successful realisation of this line requires patient work on the part of the proletariat and its organisations. They must be fully aware of the complexity of the problem and also the ability of imperialism and reaction to influence these strata.

At the same time the actions of the ultra-left against the small and middle property-owners, actions that were not opposed by all of Popular Unity, evoked a negative reaction that was far greater than the actual number of actions or the real influence of the instigators warranted. This was due to the fact that Popular Unity had no clearly defined understanding of the character of the given stage of the revolution and some people believed that this was already a full-scale socialist revolution.

Moreover, they failed to realise that even in a socialist revolution one must pursue a policy towards the middle strata that allows them to contribute to the development of the process. This policy must be broad, flexible and at the same time firm. It must be carried through by combining the material interest of these strata with persuasion and simultaneously with greater popular pressure by the masses to stop the petit-bourgeoisie from wavering.

The fact that we openly proclaim our socialist goals does not in itself restrict the scope of the working class for making alliances. In the present period, in conditions of state-monopoly capitalism that has made its appearance today even in the undeveloped countries, the contradictions between imperialism and these countries, between the financial oligarchies and the peoples are becoming more intense. The point is to reveal these contradictions and use them, as Lenin did in the setting of the Russian society of that time. This means finding formulas for broad mutual understanding and attempts to win the middle strata over to socialism by responding to their legitimate demands, ensuring them a level of income and developing forms for their participation in the new society that will induce them to make their choice in favour of this society.

All the parties of Popular Unity helped to prepare the ground for the victory of 1970 and the installation of President Allende's government. But it is also an indisputable fact that the Communist Party was the main force in making the Chilean revolution. It was the Communist Party that saw the possibility of setting up a popular government without resorting to the use of arms, and that evolved practical measures for pursuing this alternative. For this it deserves credit.

Our Party worked tirelessly for many years to rally the anti-imperialist and anti-oligarchy forces round the working class, taking into account the urgency and necessity of the changes that were long overdue in Chilean society. The Communist Party correctly defined the nature of the revolution and the policy of alliances. It reached the conclusion that the peaceful path does not rule out certain forms of coercion (such as the seizing of land by the peasants in the rural areas, and by settlement dwellers on the outskirts of cities), and that unity and the constant active mobilisation of the masses are a prime necessity.

In the campaign for full realisation of this policy, which practice proved to be correct, the Communist Party consistently opposed leftist sectarianism, which cast doubts on its policy and refused to accept the tactics of broad alliances. The Communist Party also opposed the rightists, who stood for conciliating the enemy.

The Communist Party acquired very great influence over broad sections of the working class, particularly the industrial proletariat, the miners and also the construction workers. In those years its influence quickly spread to the rural areas, particularly among the agricultural workers. The Communist Party was very strong among the young people: the country's biggest political youth organisation was the Communist Youth.

Our influence was substantial in university circles and among people working in the cultural field. It was considerably less among other middle strata. From the organisational standpoint the Communist Party was the most numerous: at the time of the putsch it had 195,000 members with various degrees of political training, and the Communist Youth with 87,000 members.

We were a powerful force that given mutual understanding with our allies was quite capable of setting the broad masses in motion, even granted the fact that in the revolutionary process the masses means not hundreds of thousands but millions of people. And they could have been roused, above all for dealing with the country's major problems, which from the point of view of the mass consciousness were already ripe for solution.

However, in situations when it proved impossible to achieve mutual understanding with other forces the Communist Party's scope for mobilising the people was limited, with the result that it mobilised only the strata that were under its direct influence.

Communist influence

There was a pronounced tendency towards political stratification in the period of popular government. The political parties carried considerable weight in the national life and their decisions guided the actions not only of their members but also of the greater part of the circles that were under their influence. It is a significant fact for an appreciation of our possibilities that during the elections the ratio of votes to party members was lower in the case of our Party than for other parties (only just over two votes per party member or member of the youth organisation). So the Communist Party considered that it was fulfilling its vanguard mission not only by strengthening its ranks, not only by increasing its influence over the masses, but also by finding ways towards mutual understanding with the Socialists and other parties of Popular Unity.

Although some changes have already occurred and others may be expected, we still seek and shall go on seeking unity with all democratic and anti-fascist (including non-fascist) forces. This means that our primary aim is to achieve mutual understanding with the Socialist Party and all other parties

of Popular Unity. In the situation as it was at the time not everything depended on us. Our scope for performing the leading role was objectively limited.
We were not always able to be the acknowledged vanguard of the working
class and the people as a whole.

As Leninism teaches, the Party's firm line, its inflexible will – particularly
at crucial moments – are also factors that stir the masses. In this field, too,
we had our failings. For instance, we did not do everything to defend the
cabinet of General Prats. His resignation was provoked in March 1973, just
at the moment when reaction had set course for a putsch and the popular
government should have maintained contact with the sections of the armed
forces that were prepared to cooperate with it.

In the specific situation that prevailed in the Chilean revolutionary process it was not enough for the Party to be inflexibly resolved to emerge from
this or that critical situation with its honour intact. Initiative and revolutionary determination are essential and sometimes of vital importance, but only
when seen through the prism of objective, concrete conditions. Otherwise
there is a danger of falling into voluntarism, wishful thinking and even
adventurism.

Whatever the specific features of the Chilean revolution – and like any
revolution it has many – not one of the fundamental theses of Marxism-
Leninism can be placed in doubt in the light of this experience. On the contrary, our experience confirms them. A deep-going and thorough analysis of
the Chilean process as a whole indicates that the general laws of revolution
remain valid. The successes we achieved were due rather to the application of
these laws, and our failures, to their underestimation.

These outweighed any successes or miscalculations in assessing the specific features, which of course must not be underestimated either. This is clear.
At the same time it would not be serious to assert, for example, that the fall
of the Popular Unity government was simply due to the fact that certain laws
were not taken into account. Nor would it be a scientific explanation merely
to say that we did not solve the problem of winning complete power, that we
did not switch in time to armed action or to make other similar assertions
that ignore the actual difficulties and pitfalls of the situation at the time, that
do not treat the question objectively, as a whole. We should recall yet again
Lenin's words that the truth is always concrete.

The August plenary meeting of our Central Committee revealed our actual mistakes and omissions and singled out two in particular. First, the Party
did a good job in charting its political line for the whole period that led up to
the partial winning of power, and for the first period of popular government.
It is clear today, however, that our line for winning complete power and moving on to the next stage of the revolution, which would have enabled us to
reach socialism, was not well enough worked out.

Second, we did not evolve a proper military policy. Since 1963 the Party
had been giving its members military training and making efforts to acquire
enough arms to defend the government that we were confident the people
would set up. But this was not enough, because our activity in this direction

was not accompanied by the main thing, namely persistent and sustained propaganda to give the popular movement a correct attitude to the military. This was essential to dispel the military's incorrect, slanderously inspired notions of the working class and Popular Unity, to bring the ideas of Marxism to people's minds in an un-distorted form. It must be admitted that the enemy, on the contrary, was continuously active in the armed forces.

People learn by their mistakes. Our Party, like other parties of Popular Unity, has already learned many lessons. The analysis is not yet complete. It is still going on and there are more lessons to be drawn from it and systematised. The people and working class of Chile are learning and will continue to learn as they assimilate this experience, and also the experience of other parties and peoples, the experience of struggle and revolutionary theory.

Some things have already become apparent. Popular Unity, which among other things has to its credit the fact that it has stood up to the test of defeat without giving way to a split, has at present formed a clearer and more definite notion of the character of the revolution, of the need to distinguish between its stages without walling them off from one another, the need to develop a policy of broad alliances, to unite all anti-fascist and non-fascist forces, including the Christian Democrats and democratic sectors of the armed forces – all this in the name of overthrowing the dictatorship and building a new democracy, forming a popular civilian-military government and again taking the road of change in the direction of socialism.

At the present time the Chilean people are becoming even more convinced that freedom does not exist as something over and above class. This is a class concept. The people have fought for it since the days of the Araucanian wars against the Spanish conquistadors. The working class, which aims at liberating not just itself but the whole of society, is fighting consistently for the freedom of the great majority and ultimately of all. But it cannot be said that in the three-year period of popular government this basic problem was tackled correctly in every way.

Our government was a major advance on the road of democratisation. It enlarged the people's freedoms and gave the working people rights and opportunities that they had never known before, such as the right to manage the enterprise where they worked. All this is undoubtedly to the credit of the popular government. But it made a grave mistake in allowing the forces of counter-revolution to enjoy almost unlimited freedom, so that they could ultimately put an end to freedom.

Popular Unity advocated and still advocates a pluralist regime that recognises guarantees also for an opposition as long as it stays within the bounds of laws passed sovereignly by the people in accordance with the norms of a legal state. We Chilean Communists stand firm on this.

We advocate a concept of pluralism in which there is no room for fascism, for a regime that is a synonym for crime that contradicts freedom. As was stated at our plenary meeting, the revolution should give the people more freedom, but none to their enemies. Our own grim experience has taught us this.

116

And one last question. For a long time the Chilean revolution was able to develop without resort to arms not only thanks to the efforts of our people but also thanks to the new international conditions, to the changes in the balance of world forces. Until quite recently not everyone fully appreciated the historical significance of the October Revolution, the role of the USSR and the countries of the socialist community, and their policy of peaceful coexistence. The advocates of decisive action sometimes showed signs of anti-Sovietism and acquired misconceptions; the policy of detente, for example, was treated by some people as a hindrance to the peoples' struggle. Today there has been a considerable evolution in their views. They have been convinced by the facts.

Today, as in the past, we continue to enjoy the invaluable support of the USSR and the socialist world. The movement of solidarity with the people of Chile has spread across all continents. Broad democratic forces are taking part in it. But there can be no doubt that the most consistent supporters are the socialist countries, with the regrettable exception of China. On the other hand, during the years of brutal repression in Chile the world has seen such important events as the victories of the peoples of Vietnam and Angola, the overthrow of the fascist dictatorship in Portugal and the collapse of the Portuguese colonial empire, the fall of the dictatorship in Greece and the disintegration of Francoism in Spain.

All this has given not just some but the whole people of Chile the chance to appreciate the significance of the Soviet Union and the socialist countries, the significance of proletarian internationalism and international solidarity. These events have convinced the mass of the Chilean people that the world is marching forward and not back.

It is on this and, of course, above all on their own struggle that the Chilean people base their confidence in victory. Our people will smash fascism, build a new, democratic system and again take the road leading to socialism on which it had already set forth in the time of President Allende.

NOTES
1 *Partido Comunista de Chile, Boletin del Exterior.* No. 26, November-December, 1977. pp 20-21. [Spanish]

Timeline of key events

1969

9 October – Popular Unity created with the support of the Socialist, Communist, Social Democratic and Radical parties, Unitary Movement for Popular Action (MAPU)and Independent Popular Action (API).

1970

4 September – Popular Unity presidential candidate Salvador Allende won 36.2% of the vote. Jorge Alessandri for the right-wing National Party received slightly under 34.9% of the vote. Christian Democrat Radomiro Tomic won 27.8%.

25 October – Right-wing officers killed the commander in chief of the Chilean army General René Schneider Chereau. He was assassinated during a botched kidnapping attempt that the plotters had hope to blame on the left thus derailing Allende's inauguration. Schneider was a "constitutionalist" and a strong opponent of military intervention against elected governments. As a result of the assassination, the retired General Roberto Viaux was jailed, and other high military officials forced into retirement, such as the head of the Navy, the generals in charge of the garrisons in Santiago and Concepcion, a general in the Air Force, and the national Chief of Police.

1971

4 April – Popular Unity coalition won just over 50% of the valid votes cast in the municipal elections. The Opposition received 49%.

1972

September – Army General Canales forced into an early retirement for urging a coup.

9 October – A strike is called by lorry company owners. The CIA supported them with US$2 million.

1973
11 March – Legislative elections: Confederation of Democracy (alliance of Christian Democrats and National Party) won 57% of the vote, Popular Unity took 43%. Denying the right the 2/3 majority needed to impeach Allende.

29 June – El Tancazo: A failed coup attempt led by Lieutenant Colonel Roberto Souper using primarily tank units against the Popular Unity government. It was successfully put down by loyal soldiers led by Army Commander-in-Chief Carlos Prats.

22 August – The Christian Democrats and the National Party members of the Chamber of Deputies vote 81 to 47 to condemn the Allende government for moving toward "totalitarian" rule. This was to be used by the coup plotters as a pretext for their actions.

23 August – General Carlos Prats resigns as Defence Minister after an altercation during a traffic accident in Santiago two months earlier, where he fired shots a civilian driver.

11 September – General Augusto Pinochet leads counter-revolutionary coup against the Popular Unity government. Allende dies in La Moneda presidential palace after its bombardment and encirclement by the army. Thousands of left-wing activists are rounded up and subjected to torture and executions.

Glossary of political parties

API
Acción Popular Independiente [Independent Popular Action]
A small Chilean political party created in 1968. It was part of the Popular Unity alliance.

Christian Democratic Party
Founded in 1957, the party's centrism saw it occasionally support co-operation with the left – supporting Allende's confirmation as president in 1970 and the nationalisation of the copper industry – and later with the right. In 1972 it allied with the right-wing National Party to contest the 1973 elections.

Christian Left
Founded in 1971 when a number of Christian Democrat MPs, the leader of the Christian Democratic youth organisation, and other supporters left in protest at the party's growing cooperation with the right-wing forces. The new organization was joined by a number of MAPU members.

Communist Party of Chile (PCCh)
Formed in 1912 as the Socialist Workers Party of Chile, it was renamed the Communist Party in 1922. It was banned several times but from the 1960s onward it worked in coalitions with the Socialist Party, culminating in the creation of Popular Unity.

El Siglo – (The Century)
Newspaper of the Communist Party of Chile.

The Confederation of Democracy
An electoral alliance of the centre and right-wing Chilean political parties formed in July 1972. Its main purpose was to unite all the opposition parties of the Popular Unity government to face the parliamentary elections on March 1973. Its main objective was to optimise the collection of votes and seats, and accomplish the majority of Congress and thus obtain at least two thirds of the deputies.

MAPU

Unitary Popular Action Movement was formed by a group of former Christian Democrats in 1969. MAPU was a signatory to the Poular Unity programme. The party suffered two splits during the Popular Unity period, one to the Christian Left and another in March 1973 with the formation of MAPU Obrero Campesino (MAPU Worker-Peasant).

MIR

The MIR (Movement of the Revolutionary Left) was a Chilean far-left political and guerrilla organization founded in 1965. The MIR was heavily influenced by the experience of the Cuban Revolution. It remained outside the Popular Unity which it viewed as reformist, while many of its own actions were criticised as adventurist Popular Unity parties particularly the Communists.

Patria y Libertad [Fatherland and Freedom]

A fascist paramilitary group active during the Popular Unity period. It received some funding from the CIA and was involved in numerous acts of violence and sabotage.

Radical Party

Founded in 1863 as a rationalist and secular party, the Radicals joined the Popular Unity alliance in 1970. The party suffered several right-wing splits during this time.

Socialist Party of Chile

Founded in 1933. Its 1967 congress redefined the party as Marxist-Leninist. The Socialist Party was one of the founding members of the Popular Unity bloc.

National Party (Partido Nacional, PN)

Founded in 1966. It represented the right-wing of the Chilean political spectrum, against the centrist Christian Democratic Party and the leftist coalition Popular Unity. It formed a joint bloc with the Christian Democrats in the 1973 legislative elections. After the September coup, which it supported, the party dissolved itself. Many of its leaders took political positions in the Pinochet regime.

OTHER PRAXIS PRESS TITLES

MEMOIRS OF A MILITANT – Kevin Halpin
One of Britain's leading communists, Kevin Halpin has been a fighter all his life. Kevin has divided his account of life through the 20th century and beyond into 15 chapters. They cover his early years in Preston; his wartime service in minesweepers; joining the Communist Party and the start of his main working life back in Britain, together with his growing Marxist education. There's a detailed examination of the impact of the historic 20th Soviet party congress and its impact on political thinking in Britain. Accounts of political activity, historic strikes, blacklisting and the crises within the communist movement spring to life as Kevin weaves through them the pithy and humorous observations of a man who was there, saw it all and understood what was happening.
ISBN 978-1-899155-05-7

HARDBOILED ACTIVIST: THE WORK AND POLITICS OF DASHIELL HAMMETT by Ken Fuller
Ken Fuller's ground-breaking work challenges those who claim to find traces of Marxism in Hammett's stories and novels, demonstrating that this was a development of the second half of the 1930s, by which time his writing career was effectively over. Fuller traces Hammett's political trajectory—from the man who believed in nothing (and therefore found life pointless) to the political activist who discovered commitment in mid-life, supporting progressive causes throughout his remaining years, choosing prison over the abandonment of his principles, and standing up to Joseph McCarthy.
ISBN: 9781899155064

Forthcoming

WHITE COLLAR: RED TIES
Professional Workers and the Communist Party of Great Britain by Dr. Steve Parsons
This book examines the reasons why middle-class intellectuals were attracted to the British Communist Party; the various cultural and political initiatives they were involved in and their changing role in the CPGB. The book analyses the way middle-class Communists drew upon their professional and technical skills to contribute to the life of the Party and its political campaigns.

MARX200
Selected papers from the 2018 London conference hosted by the Marx Memorial Library on the relevance of Marxism 200 years after the birth of Karl Marx.

Please contact praxispress@me.com for details of publication date, pricing and orders.

Lightning Source UK Ltd.
Milton Keynes UK
UKHW020614091219
355034UK00012B/1236/P